Racial Conflict and Economic Development

THE W. E. B. DU BOIS LECTURES · 1982
Sponsored by the Ford Foundation

Racial Conflict and Economic Development

W. ARTHUR LEWIS

HARVARD UNIVERSITY PRESS
Cambridge, Massachusetts, and London, England   1985

LIBRARY OF CONGRESS CATALOGING IN PUBLICATION DATA

Lewis, W. Arthur (William Arthur), 1915–
  Racial conflict and economic development.

  (The W.E.B. Du Bois lectures ; 1982)
  Bibliography: p.
  Includes index.
  1. Economic development—Addresses, essays, lectures.   2. International
economic relations—Addresses, essays, lectures.   3. Race relations—
Addresses, essays, lectures.   I. Title.   II. Series.
HD82.L4153 1985   305.8   84-25178
ISBN 0-674-74579-5 (alk. paper)

Preface

THESE W. E. B. DU BOIS LECTURES were delivered at Harvard University in the spring of 1982. "Come and give six public lectures next year on a multidisciplinary topic" is a call to reflection, rather than to research. What readers will find in this book is not a systematic treatise, but a set of topics on which I have pondered from time to time. With luck my set of interests will overlap with theirs.

Because most of my life has been lived outside the United States, my reflections are not mainly about American patterns. Two chapters (5 and 6), however, deal exclusively with the United States labor market. Two others (8 and 9) deal exclusively with the European colonies; the remaining chapters benefit, I hope, from having wider perspectives.

The subjects dealt with are highly controversial. Among the ones that have provoked a flood of books or articles in recent years are discrimination, colonialism, affirmative action, entrepreneurship, federalism, dual labor markets, multinational corporations, and the international economic order. I have attempted to discern the actual role race plays in each and to scrutinize the effect of economic trends in sometimes weakening and sometimes strengthening racial minorities.

Special thanks are due to Professor Nathan I. Huggins, who issued the invitation to deliver the lectures, and who looked after me on the days I spent at Harvard. Also special thanks to my secretary, Beverly Kidder, who prepared the manuscript with her usual meticulous care.

W. A. L.

Woodrow Wilson School
Princeton University

Contents

Racial Conflict and
Economic Development

Economic Inequality · 1

IS ECONOMIC EQUALITY necessary for social peace? From one standpoint every so-called racial conflict is sustained (or even initiated) by an economic conflict, covert or open. What poses as a conflict between a dominant and a subordinate race, we are told, is really only a way that an exploiting minority recruits supporters of its case from people with whom it has only racial ties. The proposition is somewhat doubtful. It is probably true that every dispute, racial or not, has, or acquires, some economic edge, but this is not the same as saying that all disputes originate in economic conflict, with the implication that race is not an independent source of conflict. If the economic conflict were mitigated by movement toward equality, would the racial conflict be lessened automatically?

Economic equality between groups is an unfamiliar concept that must be defined precisely. Two groups are equal in the economic sense when the proportion of persons with income above a stipulated amount is the same in both groups. For example, if 10 percent of the green group have incomes above $15,000, then blues are equal if 10 percent of blues also have incomes above $15,000. More strictly, equality at one point on the income scale is not enough; we need equality all along the line. Equality at the median and the two quartiles would be a workable compromise.

Note that I have used income instead of wealth to measure degrees of equality. Because wealth can be translated into income and income into wealth, by discounting, economists tend to reason that present value is the same whether it originates in assets or in personal income. This is not so even in economic terms. If the incomes of two men have the same present value, one earned and the other unearned, the unearned is superior because that man has leisure as well as income, and also because he has greater borrowing power. In the social sense also he is perceived to have higher status. Marxists would add that economic power is provided by the ability to invest capital, and would deduce that what matters is equality of capital assets rather than equality of income. It does not matter for my purposes which of these you choose. Equality of capital takes longer to reach than equality of income; one might perhaps take these as successive goals.

The definition of economic equality between the races is not affected by the extent of inequality within any one race; it holds, however inegalitarian the two groups may be. The definition is not met simply by prescribing equal pay for equal work. That would be met even if the top jobs were all held by one group and the bottom jobs by the other; or if one race shared the top jobs with the other, without discrimination in pay, but was not represented in the bottom jobs. Our definition requires members of both groups to be found all the way along the social scale.

On the other hand, the definition does not require that both groups be equally represented in each industry. This point is important. Members of a minority may be found to a greater extent in some industries than in others without violating economic equality—Chinese Americans in restaurants or Afro-Americans in government service—and may even dominate some industries—German Americans in brewing. They do not have to be distributed on an equal class basis in each industry. Relatively more of the better jobs in one industry may be set against relatively fewer in some other industry to give the right aggregate distribution.

Industry specialization is important to minorities. For one thing, there may be external economies enabling firms to support each other. Also some industries are easier to penetrate than others: government service is an example. It may be important even in private employment. Some successful black corporation executives feel strange because they are always the only black member of a committee of ten or less. They feel lonely and are uncertain whether or not they are being used as tokens. But if jobs were allocated proportionately with race, one in ten is what they should expect. One has to get used to belonging to a minority. Racial specialization by industry relieves this strain, but not by much.

Inequality of incomes, as I have defined it, does not necessarily imply discrimination. The two groups may differ in age, in education, in occupations, in ownership of physical assets, or in regions of residence. The ranking describes the pattern of distribution; it does not account for it. We can, however, account for the pattern if we have the data, since we can calculate what part of the group differences is the result of age, or education, or region of residence, or whatever, and insofar as these are remediable (age is not), one can institute policies that will equate educational opportunities, facilitate easy mobility out of depressed areas, and so on. Instead therefore of assessing the degree of racial equality actually achieved, one may make equality of opportunity the subject of assessment, though this raises difficulties that I shall discuss later.

Let us turn from defining economic inequality to defining race. Economic inequality correlates with class, racial, or ethnic relations. The symptoms are the same. People in the top social classes discriminate against people in the lower social classes in much the same way as one ethnic or racial group discriminates against another. They support expensive schools to which they send their children; they favor members of their own class when appointing to the better jobs; they resist interclass marriage; they zone residential areas to keep the poor out; and so on.

Let us begin with ethnicity, which runs so close to race that the two are often confused in popular speech. Race is differentiated by what is inherited genetically, most notably color of skin and texture of hair, while ethnicity differentiates what is acquired from one's culture, most notably religion and language, but also dress, eating habits, noise levels, rules of adolescent dating, or family structures. Thus, Turkish guest workers are sometimes said to be unpopular in Germany because of their race, whereas what is at work are ethnic differences.

Ethnic antagonisms provoke as much violence as racial antagonisms—more in Africa and Asia and Western Europe. They do not need the support of racial differences to inspire their unpleasantness. They are older than racial antagonisms. Ethnic tolerance has flourished best in large empires, like the Roman, the Russian, the Turkish, and the British. It is not feasible for an emperor to impose a single cultural stamp over a wide territory, so he must come to terms with the various groups under his jurisdiction. Accordingly, the decline and breakup of empires is favorable to the creation of new nation-states; each minority demands the right to secede and set up its own sovereignty. We are living in such times, starting with the disintegration of the Turkish empire, and now encompassing the world. A flood of ethnic antagonism has engulfed all the continents of the world, including places where we thought such ideas had died out decades ago, such as Belgium or Scotland.

The violence of ethnic antagonism has surprised the leaders of new states in Asia and Africa. Men like Nehru and Nkrumah grew up learning European political philosophy, where they were taught that the central mover of society is class conflict. So they were very surprised when the biggest division in their countries turned out to center around language, religion, or tribal affiliation, with which they never learned how to cope. We are still trying to piece together a political philosophy suitable for multiethnic states.

Although racial difference has a genetic base, there is no direct link between genetics and popular definitions of race. The public has decided that men of different skin color are of different races. But one could equally distinguish by the shape of the nose, the color of the eyes, the blood type, hair texture, or any other inherited characteristic. As late as the second half of the nineteenth century, anthropologists became very excited about the shape of the head, which they used to divide men into two races—dolicocephalic or longheads, and brachycephalic or broadheads—but this particular insight has died. For popular use, the distinction must be one that can be seen at a glance, so blood types or performance in various kinds of intelligence tests are not very appropriate. For the sociologist (though not for the biologist) race is in the eye of the beholder. If one must distinguish people into races, color of skin is as good as any other index, and better than most.

The definition of race is at its most anomalous when applied to persons of mixed race. Such people may be treated as a separate social group, like Anglo-Indians or like coloured persons in the Union of South Africa. Or their relations may be tilted in either direction—toward integration into the more powerful group in their heritage, as in Mexico, or toward membership in the less powerful group, like people of color in the southern part of the United States. Here the genetic and the social definitions are at their most incompatible. The causes of this wide variation of practice, especially as between the relatively liberal Spanish, French, and Portuguese, and the stricter British, Boer, and American types have not been satisfactorily established. They embrace differences between the Roman Catholic and the Protestant religions, long familiarity with the more relaxed customs of Islam, and different degrees of labor shortage; but there is no possibility at this stage of reaching unchallengeable explanations.

Racial antagonism is younger than ethnic and class antagonisms. Race seems not to have mattered much in the world until fairly recent times, that is to say, until the development of the Atlantic slave trade from the seventeenth century onward. One can of course trace incidents before this, but only of small orders of magnitude well-typified by Shakespeare's Othello, whose blackness offended a few but not most of those with whom he dealt. Even the Spanish confrontation with the Indians in South America did not produce a racist literature. The big event is the introduction of African slavery into the Americas.

An African slave trade had been in existence long before the Spaniards reached the Americas. About 10,000 slaves a year were being shipped in the fifteenth century and earlier, mostly across the Sahara to North Africa and the Middle East. The transatlantic trade soon exceeded this by a factor of six. In the next two centuries (1650–1850) about 15 million slaves were transported across the Atlantic.

A huge industry of this type had to have some ethical support. This was difficult, because Western Europe had long before outlawed slavery. The condition was not compatible with the Christian religion. To make it compatible, one had to argue that an African was in some sense not completely human and therefore not entitled to the same rights as other men. So began the massive flow of racist literature. It peaked in the United States at the end of the First World War, but continued on a high plateau, stimulated by the migration of blacks to northern cities, which migration also then became substantial. In the United States racism is now on a downward slope, as are also both ethnic antagonism and class consciousness. At the same time, ethnic antagonism has been rising in the rest of the world, as the imperial blankets are removed; and class antagonism also seems to be intensifying.

How much violence could be supported by racial differences as such, in the absence of ethnic difference, is hard to surmise, for the evidence is sparse. The evidence must come from countries where people of different races speak the same language, have the same religion, play the same games, share the same national heroes, and so on. The best example may be the United States, where the cultural differences between blacks and whites are already rather small, compared with cultural differences elsewhere—a fact that neither group likes to hear. However, attitudes are still evolving in the United States, so the time is not yet ripe for firm conclusions. Besides, the blacks are economically unequal, so the relationship is complicated by class antagonisms.

It seems reasonable to expect that cultural assimilation will reduce the likelihood of racial or ethnic explosion, but this may not be so. The dominant group, even when retreating, tends to yield its privileges slowly, while the subordinate group tends to accelerate its demands as assimilation widens its horizons and increases its need for a greater share of the middle-class jobs. India in the first half of this century illustrates this process. There probably is a stage of assimilation in which conflict increases before peaceful living side by side is achieved.

We are approaching the question with which we began. If economic conflict were moderated, say by the onset of great new opportunities for the whole community, would racial conflict be lessened automatically?

Economic inequality exacerbates a racial situation in one or other of four ways. First, it reduces the esteem in which the subordinate group is held. If members of one race hold the best jobs, or hold a disproportionately large share of private capital, they will look down on members of other races—and those that we look down on we feel free to exploit. Those beneath them will split in attitude. A great many will look up to the wealthier race and hold themselves and members of other poorer races in disdain. The situation is particularly bad where one race is disproportionately below the poverty line, since the stereotype comes to identify the entire race with dependence. In the United States the blacks and the very poor are identified; both black and white leaders speak continually as if this were so. I guess that this is one reason why President Reagan has met so little opposition to his attacks on the poor. Many white people believe that what he is doing affects mostly blacks, and can therefore be justified, whereas in truth blacks constitute only about a third of Americans below the poverty line.

The second effect of economic inequality on a racial situation is that it facilitates exploitation by blunting weapons that the subordinate group could otherwise use to increase its bargaining power. In other words, for lack of money and influence the subordinate group receives too little schooling, land, infrastructure, irrigation water, credit facilities, and so on, by comparison with what is available to members of the dominant group. So it falls further behind. If economic equality prevailed, members of each race would be participating at all social levels, and the racial tensions would be muted.

Third, economic inequality adds envy to racial differences. For example, many peoples have lived side by side in the Middle East for a very long time in relative harmony. It was common practice for a group to specialize in one of a small number of industries or occupations. Then, as Charles Issawi sees it, when the Industrial Revolution came along in the nineteenth century, benefiting some industries and therefore some ethnic groups while impoverishing others, harmony gave place to conflict. Similarly, hostility toward Chinese in Southeast Asia or toward Indians in East Africa would be less intense were it not for the specialization of these groups in trade. I noted before some reasons why minorities tend to specialize; now we see that it is sometimes better to keep a low profile.

We meet the fourth contribution of economic inequality where the subordinate class is itself racially divided, so that employers or traders or landlords can manipulate one group against another—in strikebreaking, in defeating boycotts, or in other industrial action. Working-class leaders on either side of the racial fence are then perplexed as to what action they should take. They themselves may see joint action by their members as the right strategy, but it may not be feasible if their members have been indoctrinated with racism. Similar problems arise when people of different religious, language, or tribal groups form their own trade unions.

Race also serves more generally as a tool of exploitation, maintaining an abundant supply of unskilled labor, while at the same time offering the low income of the subordinate group as evidence that it could not use more freedom intelligently. This purpose is now served as well or better by class distinctions as by race. In one sense race is becoming a superfluous distinction in the United States, because whatever purpose it was invented to serve—whether exploitation or discrimination—is served by ethnic and class distinctions; and the specific occasion of its expansion, the plantation system in America, has now expired. Race was necessary to the plantation system because it defined at sight those whose labor belonged to a master. In an industrial system the employer is interested in people's skills. Race is relevant where it is used by employers for strikebreaking, but the United States has passed that stage. It is also relevant if white workers can use it as a tool to restrict the numbers eligible for entry into better-paid jobs.

Is it race that determines the intensity of economic conflict or is it the intensity of economic conflict that determines the degree of racism (for example, of denial of voting rights or segregation in housing, schooling, or public places)? If racism is dominant, then one must attack the psychological roots of racism, which would survive even if income were equalized. Whereas, if the economy is dominant, then it would be in the marketplace that economic forces would ultimately bring the whole structure of racism crumbling down. Such polarization seems unnecessary. Given the nature of human societies, mutual interdependence seems more likely than unilinear domination. Economic equality is a necessary but not a sufficient condition for racial peace. The psychological roots of racism have also to be destroyed directly, as well as by indirect economic and political action.

Interracial Goals · 2

IN THIS BOOK it is taken for granted, as a desirable goal, that members of different races should live together in peace. I have already defined economic equality between races as one condition of that peace. Another set of conditions turns on how far race should enter into public decisions about individuals. Leaders committed to the achievement of interracial peace have suggested three separate approaches, arguing respectively for what I shall refer to as the homogeneous state, the raceless state, and the plural society.

The racially homogeneous approach proposes a separate state for each race. Its advocates are pessimists who doubt that different races can live together in peace under a single government. Included here are some of the big questions of the day, such as the right of minorities to secede, the expulsion of minority communities, and the control of immigration.

Advocates of the homogeneous state see virtue in policies that recognize and enforce the rights of the dominant group.

In the raceless society race does not enter into public consideration. Equality of opportunity and equality before the law are therefore enshrined, not necessarily as between one class and another, but as between one race and another.

Each racial or ethnic group in the plural society has its own institutions, recognized as such by law or custom. The term "plural society" is somewhat confusing. It was invented by political scientists to refer to a state of limited powers that allows other social institutions, such as the church, the sports hierarchy, and the school system, to make their own decisions. But sociologists now apply it to a country with different ethnic or racial groups—that is, a multiracial or multiethnic society—and I shall use it in this sense. In the ideal plural state, the goal is "separate but equal." The phrase has become infamous because of its abuse by authorities who enforced separateness without providing for equality. But it would be a mistake to identify segregation with dominant groups, for the right to be allowed to do their own thing is the dream of many minority groups.

Each of the three ideal conditions—the homogeneous society, the raceless society, and the plural society—has ardent supporters who reject the alternatives as inappropriate for their group. Afro-Americans have had leaders pointing in each of these directions. Marcus Garvey believed in the homogeneous state; he wanted to lead black people back to Africa. (His descendants are the Rastafarians of the English-speaking Caribbean and the larger American cities.) Du Bois wanted the raceless state, as did Martin Luther King, Jr.; it has become the main thrust of the civil rights movement. The third goal, self-segregation, has no organization or numbers comparable with those of Garvey or Du Bois, but its traces can be seen quite widely, for example, in the universities, in politics, and in the original version of the Black Muslims. One lesson to be learned from the American situation is that every political proposition will find supporters.

Because racial situations are very different, we must not expect that any one of these three goals will prove appropriate for all countries. Interracial situations vary in their dimensions. One dimension is concerned with dominance. There may be a dominant and a subordinate group, or also an intermediate group, like the Indians in East Africa. Or groups may live together without dominance or subordination, as in the multinational states of Nigeria or Kenya. Another dimension is that of relative size. Subordinate groups may run from 1 percent, like colored minorities in Britain, to 99 percent, like the typical colonial situation without white settlers. (All subordinate groups are not minorities; this is a confusion common in the United States, where, for example, women are sometimes called a minority.) Similarly, the dominant group may run from 1 to 99 percent—though if there are only two groups, this statement is already implicit in saying that subordinate groups may run from 1 to 99 percent. Another important dimension of a multiracial society is whether housing is racially segregated or whether individual members of a subordinate group live all over the place. This is particularly important in regard to voting power, to schools, and to the quality of infrastructure.

Racially homogeneous societies came into existence in ancient times as a normal by-product of military conquest. One defeated a neighboring country, massacred its soldiers, carried off its younger women, imposed one's religion and language, and within a century the separate ethnicities had disappeared. This was not universal; as I have said, the big empires had to live with toleration; but the smaller states were more ruthless.

Genocide did not end in ancient times; attempts to wipe out whole peoples continued into our century, including the aboriginal peoples of the Americas and Australasia, some of the peoples of the Turkish Empire, some in the Soviet Union, and the Jews of Europe. Such actions are now universally condemned. Homogeneous states are more likely to come into existence in the opposite way. A large empire or state comprised of persons of different religions, tribes, races, or languages breaks up into several states, on the basis more or less of one nation: one state. The tide has run strongly in this direction over the past hundred years, with liberal philosophers on both sides. Some back secession, others try to persuade groups of independent states to link themselves in some kind of federation.

Three sets of arguments favor the federal solution when it is feasible: military, civil rights, and economies of scale. The military argument, put simply, is that there will be a lot more fighting if an area is divided into many small states than if military force is monopolized by one central government. This is probably the best argument for holding India together, even though centralizing the government of such a large area probably inhibits its development. On the other hand, some of the bitterest wars have incurred inside federations, including the United States and Nigeria, so the argument must not be conducted in absolutes.

The second case for the federal solution is that a central government protects civil rights better than would its constituent states. The United States is the supreme example of this. I have always thought it to be the strongest part of the case for West Indian federation, and events there since the collapse of the federation have strengthened my opinion.

The third argument for maintaining as large a country as possible is the economies of scale, and protagonists hope that this advantage will be large enough to override racial or ethnic conflicts. But in practice the major obstacle often turns out to be economic. In a country or set of neighboring countries some districts or provinces are ahead of the others and moving faster, perhaps because they have been better endowed with minerals, water, soils, human skills, or commercial traditions and institutions. These districts become growth poles, growing at the expense of the others by attracting away their scarce skills, entrepreneurship, and capital. The result is much the same whether the countries are participants in a federation or a customs union. The aggrieved districts will begin to think and act in terms of secession or of abrogation of the customs union. Jamaican fears that the West Indian federation would have this effect at its expense in favor of Trinidad played some part in bringing down the West Indian federation; though the fact that the governments almost immediately moved into a customs union suggest that this was more a political ploy than an expectation of economic substance. In these days of inflamed ethnicity, the economic argument tends to be used against groups living together, in federations or customs unions, rather than in favor.

Expulsion of people from their homes has never been acceptable to those concerned about civil rights. Our century has had plenty of cases, from the Armenians in Turkey to the Nigerians in Ghana, the Ghanaians in Nigeria, and the Indians in Uganda. Oddly enough, some minorities, like the Mennonites, have removed themselves. Marcus Garvey wanted American blacks to do that, though where they were to go was never precisely established. Undoubtedly many more groups would leave if they had a place to go.

Where ethnic cleavages are strong, partition is probably the best solution, if it can be done without leaving too many people on the wrong side of the border. Partition is not, however, a feasible solution if members of the minority are widely scattered and are everywhere a minority. One is surprised that it was ever suggested for the blacks in the United States. Nor is partition a solution on South African terms, where the whites are to live in rich, exclusive areas, and the blacks are to live in areas not capable of comparable development; the blacks commuting to work in the white areas, where they will have no political rights. As I said at the beginning, economic equality between the races is one of the conditions of peace.

If partition cannot be effected equitably and without leaving too many people on the wrong side of the border, the racially homogeneous society is not attainable. One must look to the raceless society or to the plural society for interracial solutions.

Small numbers.on the wrong side of the border need not be inconsistent with the goal of racial homogeneity. The degree of racial antagonism is an increasing function of the relative size of the minority. There is little racism if the minority is less than 1 percent of the population, especially if it is dispersed geographically and up and down the occupational scale, since it is then least visible. A minority at the bottom of the scale, like Asians in England before 1950, tends to be despised, but not persecuted. A minority at the top of the scale, such as white men in the British West Indies, is more precarious because it is accustomed to having the best jobs reserved for its children. But although the economic system can find top jobs for all whites when whites are only 1 percent of the population, it cannot do this for 5 percent. The same applies to the immigrant communities of East and West Africa. Minorities cannot survive if they need a disproportionate share of the jobs in the top 10 percent of the labor force—not after a country has become independent, and its high schools and universities have started to pour out graduates. The minority must then take jobs all the way along the social scale, like the "petits blancs" in French West Africa, or emigrate, as the West Indian whites are doing.

A small minority is also manageable because it can be assimilated through interracial mating, as a result of which it ultimately virtually disappears. The speed of this outcome depends on where the color line is drawn. Is it easy to pass for white, as it is in New York, or does the state count great-grandparents meticulously in search of the smallest blemish, as in South Africa? Are people of mixed race white, black, or a separate guild governed by different laws? As the German Jews said of Hitler's laws: A Jew is any person who a non-Jew thinks is a Jew. If it is easy for people of mixed race to pass, and if immigration is strictly controlled, in a few generations the community will be virtually homogeneous, as Mexico is on its way to becoming 100 percent mestizo. Some people believe that as the cultural assimilation of the blacks in the United States is completed, it will be followed at a slower pace by their racial integration. This, however, seems doubtful because the numbers are so large.

The homogeneous society has been the goal of many statesmen. Thus, the United States began to exclude Chinese immigrants in 1882, Japanese in 1907. Australia has kept out Asians and other colored persons; Britain claims that it is only limiting its population but has so written its immigration laws that they admit whites and exclude Africans and Asians. African and Asian governments also practice selective immigration. However the immigration law may read, race is an element in its administration in practically every country in the world.

Europeans have been able to maintain racial homogeneity in their homelands during the past five centuries because they were spilling out into the rest of the world. They annexed the temperate parts of the world that were sparsely occupied, especially the Americas and Australia, killed off most of their non-European inhabitants, and closed their doors to immigrants of other races. Into the empty tropical parts of the world, including the southern United States, they brought Africans, Indians, and Chinese, creating problems of racial accommodation that will remain with us for decades.

The current division of the world between white and colored races is menaced on two fronts. One is the attraction that the high living standards of the developed countries exert upon mass immigrants from the developing countries, because of greater opportunities for remunerative employment, better schooling for children, better medical facilities, better housing, welfare safety nets, and so on. The other threatening front is the world food situation. The developing countries can learn to feed themselves over the next twenty or thirty years, but it is not certain that they will do so. We cannot therefore exclude the possibility of massive migrations in search of food.

In the raceless society people of more than one race live together, but race is not a factor in decisions about individuals. A man is not concerned about his neighbor's religion; intermarriage excites no comment; and jobs are distributed without regard to race. Opportunities are equal, so presumably after a while all races are distributed in the same proportions along the income curve.

There are two obstacles: the forces making for separateness may be as powerful as those producing national unity; and equality of opportunity does not necessarily produce equality of result. Forces leading to separateness operate on both sides. The majority has to learn to tolerate the differences of the minority, and the minority has to learn to be willing to assimilate. Take, for example, the majority's attitude toward the minority's religion. The attainment of toleration within the Christian religion took four centuries and came about only because substantial numbers of influential people ceased to believe in religion. Outside the Christian countries people still fight and die because of religion, though the same process is beginning to occur everywhere, as agnosticism brings toleration in its train (except perhaps in parts of the Muslim world).

The most turbulent issue in many would-be raceless states today is the promotion and use of a national language. The homogeneous state recognizes only one language in government, business, and the school system; at the other extreme, the plural society may recognize several. Where does the raceless society stand? The test is usually whether the state will finance schooling in the minority languages, or at least finance schools that treat the majority language as a second language. It is claimed that such schooling allows the less gifted, minority-speaking students to benefit more from their schooling than if they were taught only or mainly in the majority language. For the more gifted students, teaching the official language as a second language seems to be a drawback. The minority-speaking student will have to pass examinations in the official language, and whether he or she goes on into government service, private industry, or the university, he or she will be competing with members of the majority, whose language facility is greater. The bilingual system, therefore, is not consistent with group economic equality. It would be consistent in a plural society, where government and business were conducted in regional languages, but not in a country with only one official language.

The demand for the use of minority languages in the schools, once granted, becomes a spearhead for the demand for the use of these languages in business and government, to even up competition. We can see the process at work in Quebec. Equality of language then becomes the thin edge of the wedge that leads to the plural society. We shall probably also see the process at work in the United States. In the nineteenth century the United States received people speaking many languages but insisted that to become citizens they must acquire American characteristics, of which the most important were the ability to speak English and an acceptance that English would be the first language of one's descendants. This policy succeeded. Now the Spanish-speaking peoples are arriving and they are demanding a different contract.

A raceless society cannot be sustained if the members of a minority group are forever yearning for the conditions that they would have in a plural society, including their own reservations, languages, schools, political organizations, and such. Whether minority leaders go in this direction, or toward the homogeneous society probably depends on past treatment. If the past has been discriminatory, as for the Catholic Irish, it will have left an irreconcilable bitterness. But even if the past has been favorable, as for the Scots, who have held every conceivable office in Britain up to and including the monarchy, loud voices can still be heard at every election demanding separateness. Whether one sees oneself as a member of a minority or as a raceless person, and is seen as such by others, is in the marginal cases a matter of sentiment no less than of actual treatment.

Let me return to the second menace to the stability of the raceless society; that equality of economic opportunity between groups does not in fact lead to equality of results, but may increase economic inequality. Normally the competitive market reduces differentials and is the best friend of the underdog. Firms that sell in a competitive market have to cut costs and will hire more black labor than firms in protected markets. If blacks have an opportunity to compete in the labor market they will get more and better jobs. Similarly, farmers get lower prices for their crops when required to sell to government marketing boards; and so on.

But there are two cases when the market works the other way; both depend on the working of cumulative forces. One involves regional competition. A country does not develop at the same pace everywhere at the same time. Some regions may become "growth poles," expanding excessively at the expense of other sections of the country because they are attracting capital, skill, and entrepreneurship from the rest. These regional disparities are very marked; the ratio of per-capita incomes reaches as much as 5:1 in some developing countries. Where the expansion (or contraction) is taking place on lands occupied by a particular group, such disparities become racial or ethnic differences. Under such circumstances it may sometimes be desirable to levy taxes in the affluent area, using the proceeds to develop less fortunate regions. Both the economics and the politics of such measures are arguable. When in the 1950s Nkrumah adopted this policy, he overdid it, and it helped to unseat him.

The other example where the cumulative forces are detrimental to equality is in competition between the children of different social classes. It is now commonplace that in school examinations the median performance is higher in the middle-class group than in the working-class group. Other differences include attitudes toward supervisory responsibility. Most psychologists agree that these differences are cultural. But whereas some can be remedied simply by providing more years of schooling (for example, in Head Start programs), others require a couple of generations.

Consequently, where middle- and working-class children take the same examinations, differences in performance do not correspond to differences in innate ability. If one is seeking to reward innate ability, one must either devise culture-free tests or rank the two groups separately. The purpose of some examinations, however, is not to reward innate ability but to predict future performance, whether in examinations or in a skill or profession. This is where the hard problems begin.

It is in the interest of the black population that its work be done by competent persons, whether black or white: that its surgeons be as good as any others; that its bridges do not collapse because of incompetent design; that the mechanics who repair its television sets know what they are doing—and so on, all along the line. There can be no compromise on examinations for admitting persons into professions and skills. All such tests must be color-blind.

Admission to training is a different matter, especially where the handicaps of background can be overcome by fitting an extra remedial year into the curriculum. Supplementation of entrance examination results with other data is then desirable in either of two cases. First, if innate ability is what one is seeking and the examination results give erroneous rankings. Good faith is indicated by applying this supplementation to all disadvantaged candidates of whatever race, for example, by reserving one-third of the entrance places for students whose parental income does not exceed x thousand dollars a year. Thus, the white disadvantaged also get a fairer share.

The second situation is the plural society, where groups live side by side, but within their own institutions and with separate leadership. Here it makes sense to say: "We shall ensure post-secondary education for the top 5 percent of each group. Whether we like it or not, these people are going to be the leaders of subordinate groups with which we must constantly negotiate and come to terms." As they are reported as saying in Oxford and Cambridge, we must educate our masters. The belief that higher education exists only to produce intellectuals is false. However, because of extra remedial schooling, this policy will entail relatively heavier expenditure on the less advanced groups. This is part of the price that the more advanced must pay for moving toward economic equality and interethnic tranquility.

This argument is not peculiar to the United States. It is relevant to taxes paid by Indians in East Africa that support schools for African children, to Chinese-Malay relations in Malaysia, to education in Northern Nigeria, and so on. The argument postulates good faith; it sets up equality of innate ability as the test of admission and could not be used to justify excluding from the local university middle class or white or Chinese students whose innate ability exceeds that of other students who are admitted. I recognize that these arguments can easily be overstated. Working-class people and minority groups have lifted themselves by their own bootstraps in many parts of the world without special action on their behalf—Japanese in America, Ibos in Nigeria, and workers' and farmers' children everywhere. But to say that some progress will occur even without special action is not to deny that special action may be appropriate.

Beyond the problems of training lie those of employment. In the first place, the labor market is very imperfect. Young disadvantaged persons do not know what jobs are available, and employers need help in recruiting and accommodating members of unfamiliar groups. In the United States young blacks are particularly disadvantaged with regard to employment in the more worthwhile jobs involving skill and in-service training, partly because most of these jobs are filled through recommendations by other workers and partly because of sheer prejudice. If blacks are to obtain a fair share of such jobs, outside pressure must be applied to employers, countering ignorance, inertia, or pressure in the reverse direction.

Remedial pressure takes the form of requiring of an employer over the next n years that at least x percent of his hirings in category A and y percent in category B shall be members of the disadvantaged group, where the x's and the y's are based on the numbers of qualified disadvantaged expected to be in the market. Some such legislation is now commonplace in developing countries, where it is applied to foreign employers by requiring them to have work permits for their expatriate staff. India is a special case, because the government has applied such legislation even to itself, in reserving a quota of jobs for the scheduled castes. U.S. government measures providing for a minimum minority share in government contracts are in principle the same.

Many employers welcome this sort of legislation, which enables them to resist pressures from their own employees and others to discriminate against minorities. Quotas not based on currently available qualified persons are unreasonable, but realistic quotas based on numbers available protect both employer and employee against prejudice.

To sum up, the raceless society is not feasible unless both majority and minority parties wish to live together on such terms; it also tends to move away from economic equality unless supported by affirmative action. The system can be made to work, but this requires continual effort.

So we come to the third alternative goal, the plural society. Here the leaders of minority groups are demanding separate treatment by the law. This seems strange to members of societies whose self-image is homogeneous or raceless, because in such societies the minorities are struggling to break down segregation and to be incorporated into the general body. But even there it is not unusual for minority spokesmen to be seeking self-segregation. The next greatest area of segregation in the United States, after the Christian church, is the liberal arts college, and this is the work of black students' overriding white administrations.

A plural system can be achieved if the groups involved have a strong desire to govern themselves, not necessarily as sovereign states but to the limits of the federal system. This is possible where members of the minority live together, especially if they are all in one geographical location. It becomes less feasible if within this location live other persons, who would become a minority within a minority; or if the group lives not in one location but in several. It is not feasible at all if the minority is scattered throughout the country; here the raceless society is the only reasonable goal.

The plural system minimizes movement toward economic equality, if indeed it does not promote greater inequality. As we have seen, some provinces develop more rapidly than others, and it is normal in centralized states to let the rich provinces subsidize the infrastructure of the poor provinces. Federal systems circumscribe the right of the center to tax and to spend. The gap between rich and poor provinces is thus widened.

On the subject of geographical segregation, minority leaders look both ways. They want their people to be free to segregate themselves, but not to be forced to do so. It is not improper for there to be tribal reservations, lands available only to members of the tribe—provided that members of the tribe who wish to live elsewhere are free to do so. Urban housing raises similar issues. Blacks are segregated in the United States by obstacles impeding their buying property in "white areas." Black leaders attack such segregation but would be disconcerted if it came to an end, for there then would be less chance of black voters' electing black politicians to Congress—though the politicians might have more influence in some closely disputed constituencies.

Segregated housing leads to segregated schooling, another heated American issue. The case against separate schools in the United States is that the schools provided are separate but unequal. Thus, the only way to achieve justice for black children is to have black and white in the same school. But in other countries separate schools are not inherently unequal; in fact they are inevitable where the children speak different languages. It is not uncommon for tribal or religious authorities to provide their own schools, subsidized by the government.

School segregation with local control opens the door to the objective of another set of tribal leaders, those who wish to preserve a separate minority culture and way of life. This almost always means the playing down of science in education, in favor of emphasis on literature, history, and handicrafts. It almost always results in relatively low average performance of the students on national tests and examinations. And further, it results in lower achievement in the scientific professions. These things are not inevitable. The preservation of cultural values is not incompatible with learning mathematics; it just seems to work that way, except in groups with long intellectual traditions like those of the Japanese or the Jews.

Nor is the preservation of cultural values incompatible with preserving civil liberties, though nationalist movements have tended to head in the opposite direction. Young people should not, in the name of cultural purity, be prevented from living where they will, from studying in universities that are not ethnically inclined, from marrying whom they like, from emigrating, or even from "passing." Dissenters will have a hard time, since ethnicity feeds upon itself, offering affection and status where the outside world offers hostility and contempt. A plan for an ideal plural society must include the normal liberties of the individual.

Social systems that downgrade science and technology are in the long run unstable. The young people trained within such a system, and finding it a handicap when they try to compete in the outside world, will turn against it if only for their children's sake. The case of French Quebec reminds us that this revolt may take several generations to come to the boil, but nowadays such reactions are speeded up. The plural society is the talking point of our day, because there are so many new countries where the right of component groups to do their own thing is a condition for holding the nation together. To those of us brought up in countries with homogeneous or raceless goals it seems a queer phenomenon, not yielding its secrets to our established political philosophies. As a long-run goal, it is probably inferior to the alternatives, because it keeps group differences alive and probably moves away from rather than toward group economic equality. But as a short-run refuge from cleavage and strife, it is in many places the best that we can do for the time being.

Investment in Underdeveloped Groups · 3

WHY DOES a ruling group exploit and impoverish a subordinate group when it could profit by developing the potential of the subordinate group? Why do not white South Africans, for example, invest more in raising the skills of black South Africans, instead of holding them down? Why do not Indian landowners invest more in the irrigation and infrastructure of their villages? Would it pay the developed countries to make grants toward (or otherwise subsidize) economic projects in the poorer countries?

There are three answers: the yield of investment in subordinate groups may be exaggerated; the yield from exploitation may exceed that from development; and the fruit of investment, even when plentiful, does not necessarily accrue to the investor.

The yield of investment in subordinate groups is frequently exaggerated. Most statements of the case include a transfer element, which is a mistake. The argument runs as follows: If employers paid higher wages the workers would buy more; so the market would be larger, profits would be higher, there would be more investment, and the economy would be more prosperous. It is true that the workers would have more, but the employers would therefore reap smaller profits; they would invest less and the system would contract. The kind of increase in real wages that causes the system to expand is an increase resulting from increased productivity. This fruit can be shared by worker and employer.

Of course transfers can also be productive. If workers or peasants are undernourished, transfers of food may raise their productivity. Anything that raises productivity is theoretically capable of benefiting both parties. Insofar as we are talking about the dominant group benefiting from the higher earnings of the subordinate group, we are talking about productivity, not just about transfers.

Expectations from education are also exaggerated. The vast econometric literature on this subject has not turned out to be all that helpful. It is useful when we are studying the private return to education—the extra yield to the individual of extra years of schooling—but it is not so helpful in studying the social rate of return, for many reasons, the most important of which for us is that in markets where discrimination is institutionalized, differences between earnings do not necessarily reflect the real social value of different kinds of work.

Econometrics aside, the economic productivity of education tends to be exaggerated by dwelling on the importance of the work of educated persons, while forgetting how few such persons can be absorbed into a community where 70 percent of the population is engaged in small-scale agriculture. Because agriculture absorbs very few persons with completed high school education, such an economy has difficulty in providing high school jobs for more than 5 percent of the cohort, or college jobs for more than 1 percent. As India has discovered, even doctors, engineers, and chemists can be easily overproduced—not to mention graduates in literature and the social sciences. Overproduction is not confined to the university level. Overproduction of secondary school graduates is now common in developing countries. West Africa even demonstrates overproduction of primary school graduates, in the sense that there is a shortage of the types of jobs that those who have attended primary school expect to get, so that they are increasingly unemployed.

None of this discounts the cultural or political value of education or challenges the right of all young people to attend school. But the economic benefits of schooling have been exaggerated, except insofar as the expansion of schooling and absorptive capacity keep pace with each other. This is not to deny that there are real and substantial economic benefits within the limits of absorptive capacity, nor to deny the relevance of other social and personal gains. Our concern in this context is only with the yield from the investment.

This is a function of absorptive capacity, itself a function of place and time. Investment of any kind (education has served only as a proxy in this argument) must be related to what is happening simultaneously in the economy that will facilitate its absorption and usefulness. Place is relevant, since some locations have greater absorptive capacity than others—richly watered soil, minerals, a stock of skilled persons, a stable government, and so on. Time, too, is relevant, because conditions change.

We must recognize that it is not true everywhere that investments in physical or human capital will yield abundant fruit in the near future. I am not arguing that aid should be given only to countries with excellent economic prospects. Aid has its own rules, which provide for helping some of those who cannot help themselves. Our current concern is only with yield.

Finally, we have also to recognize the impressive productivity of underdeveloped countries, one-third of which were growing in the 1960s and 1970s at not less than 3 percent per head per year. Money invested in that group had about the same capital output ratio as money invested at home in the developed countries. If there was a deficit of capital expenditure, it was not from a lack of absorptive capacity or insufficient yield.

Although the yield is high by, say, West European standards, it is not as high as the gain available from various forms of exploitation: such as when immigrants kill the aborigines and seize their lands; purchase slaves and force them to work; levy taxes on villagers payable only in cash, thus forcing them to work in the mines; or prevent villagers from growing export crops (or levy heavy taxes on export crops) to force them to work for employers; and so on.

No useful purpose would be served by trying to calculate benefit cost ratios for such exercises. For one thing, their perpetrators were not driven by such calculations; they were driven by fear and ignorance and the pleasure some people get from inflicting pain or death upon other people.

There is no reason to doubt that under certain circumstances forms of enslavement are more profitable to the slaveholders than systems of free enterprise. If there were to be a presumption, it would turn on the remarkable characteristics of compound interest. Enslavement practices frequently result in declining output per head, while the investments we are concerned with result in increasing output per head—possibly doubling agricultural output every thirty-five years. Other things being equal, a landlord should always prefer to see his tenants getting richer, unless in the process their bargaining power against him is significantly strengthened.

Extreme forms of predatory behavior have almost completely disappeared, so it is more profitable to consider cases where farmers and landlords live side by side without overt force, as in the Indian countryside today, or the southern states around 1950, when there were still considerable numbers of black farmers. Given that the opportunities for innovation exist, why do not landowners invest more in improving the countryside? It was under such conditions that progressive landlords in Western Europe reformed agricultural practice in the eighteenth and nineteenth centuries. What prevents this in the less-developed countries today?

The answer turns on externalities: the profit from an investment need not necessarily return to the investor. The effort of one landowner acting independently may be ineffective. The improvements under his control must be supported by other investments by other investors in the chain—middlemen, processors, moneylenders, those who control irrigation water, and others. Much emphasis is placed on this need for cooperative action, and the point has substance even when stripped of the rhetoric of coordinated planning.

Even if one landowner could make an effective program by himself, where the returns would clearly exceed the cost, he would be inhibited from proceeding unless he could count on capturing his share of the result. An investment can be highly profitable overall, yet be unprofitable to the investor. Revenues may accrue through different channels—taxes, trade, profits or interest on loans—requiring participation of the entire business community. To make progress requires bringing together all or most of those who will benefit and getting their commitment to contribute. This is hard to achieve. As students of cartels have taught us, it is to the benefit of each seller that there should be a cartel—so long as he is not a member. Programs involving externalities have to be left to the government, and governments composed of landowners are slow to act.

The backwash effects may also be substantial. One effect of raising farm productivity will be higher wages, and landowners will not like this. Another example, an offshoot of rural schooling, is the stimulation of migration to the towns; this also raises wages. Thus, from the end of the Civil War to the end of the First World War the economy of the rural South in the United States was based on low wages associated with low skills and low mobility. Progressive policies would doubtless have raised the standard of living, but many powerful landowners must have feared that this would be at their expense.

Given the wide extent of required agricultural programs, the significance of externalities and the difficulties of securing joint action in such programs, the questions remains: Why, since greater productivity would yield higher rents, do not the landlords of, say, India take the lead in agrarian reform, as their Dutch counterparts did in the nineteenth century? One answer is that we do not have the detail that would show whether the opportunities really are comparable. The second is that some Indian landowners do in fact invest in their tenants; we just do not know how their numbers compare with the Dutch landowners. And the third answer is that Indian landlords are not Dutch. Their outlook is not the same, and the fundamental assumption of economists that if some new course of action is profitable it is going to be adopted is true neither of the one group nor of the other. The Dutch changed in the course of the nineteenth century in ways that the Indian landowners are now adopting only in the second half of the twentieth century.

This line of argument applies mutatis mutandis to industrial expansion. Just as it would pay the landowner to have more skilled and productive farmers, so it pays the industrialist to be able to hire more skilled and productive employees. Both lose from mere transfers of income from themselves to their tenants or employees, but both gain by paying more for greater skill. Both have physical constraints on the rate of growth of output, stemming in agriculture from shortage of the most fertile land, and in industry from the time taken for interindustrial coordination in a market system. Both are constrained by need for balanced growth. Industry must dispose of a product growing at 7 percent a year or more; it either sells at home to a market of expanding farm surpluses and service incomes or else faces the need to export manufactures with rapid growth. Agriculture will go bankrupt if its expanding output cannot be taken up by an expanding urban population or by exports.

The industrial system can expand at any speed consistent with the evolution of home and export demands. It can take a fast growth path, with high investment, high saving, a high profits ratio, an insatiable demand for labor, rapid growth of exports, and fast increases in productivity and real wages. Germany and Japan are on such paths. Labor does not constrain Germany's industrial sector, which imports it, nor that of Japan, which is still running down its reservoirs of surplus labor. Or the system can have relatively lower saving, investment, and profits, with slower increases in productivity and real wages and a tendency to long spells of unemployment. The United States and Britain are on such paths. The same country can cross from one path to another. If wages rise faster than productivity, the country will move to a slower growth path; if wages rise more slowly, then it moves to a higher growth path, where services and public construction move the balance toward more intensive use of capital. The country with the lower wage ratio and faster growth will soon overtake and pass the wage level of the country with the higher wage ratio and slower growth.

It follows that industrialists as a group have nothing to fear from measures that raise the productivity of their workers, if the economy is growing fast and flexibly. If the manufacturing sector is to grow rapidly, other sectors must do the same, though at different speeds according to their differing elasticities of demand and supply. If the system is not flexible enough, losses in some sectors will slow it down, even though matched by excess profits elsewhere; hence the fear that the growth of productivity may cause unemployment. By now the advanced industrial countries of Western Europe have become flexible enough to adjust to major structural changes. This is the lesson of the 1950s and the 1960s. Part of that flexibility derives from industrial training; part derives from bold use of international trade to eliminate surpluses and deficits of individual commodities, thereby doing away with the need for domestic balance. Given this background, as a group the industrial countries have nothing to fear from measures that raise the productivity of their workers—though it remains true that individually some have more to fear than others.

As for the workers, their interest lies in maintaining full employment, which depends on high levels of investment, which depend on rising productivity. Nineteenth-century economists worried about the apparent clash between employment and productivity, mainly because they underestimated the potential amount of investment. Yet, throughout that century, employment kept up not only with productivity but also with population growth, despite what we now regard as rather low levels of investment per decade. The problem we face today is how to keep the system growing fast enough, with its various elements, including foreign trade, in mutual balance. We are not yet expert at doing this, but our expertise is not facilitated by keeping productivity low. This much is understood in modern industrial societies, though it is still to penetrate the world-image of holdovers from the nineteenth century.

We may therefore deduce that while employers will not be averse to holding down wages of any group of workers, white or black, in pursuit of transfers from wages to profits, they will not favor measures that retard the productivity and skill formation of potential employees. Measures that minimize the pool of skilled labor will seem particularly obnoxious, because they hold down the growth rate of the economy and the level of profits.

An examination of the case for financial subsidies from developed to developing countries must begin by eliminating a couple of fallacies. That "the money returns to the developed countries" is irrelevant; the goods and services remain in the developing countries. Also irrelevant is the Keynesian argument that expenditure in the less-developed countries (LDCs) will stimulate production and exports in the industrial countries; this stimulus would follow equally from expenditure at home.

Leaving these fallacies aside, we note that financial subsidies pass the test that the yield of investment is as high in LDC's as in MDCs (more-developed countries), subject to the periodic bouts of rescheduling, suspension, and default that have been a regular feature of international lending since the 1820s. These transfers meet the further test that MDCs as a whole will capture the externalities, even if individual aid donor countries may not do so.

The principal financial benefit to MDCs, apart from interest and dividend payments, is that investment in agriculture or in mining will swing the terms of trade in favor of MDCs. Manufacturing is a more complex case. LDC production at the margin will be of low-range goods for export. The importation of these into MDCs will create unemployment there. However, the LDC export of low-wage munufactures is presumably associated with additional LDC imports of high-wage manufactures. So in the MDCs labor is transferred out of low-wage into high-wage manufacturing. This is a net gain for the MDCs, except insofar as they fail to make the transfers.

A further gain is possible if high-wage industries in MDCs are subject to economies of scale, which come to fruition as LDC demand expands. This seems obvious, but it is not in fact quite clear. Some industrial countries will surge ahead, while others may find it harder to grow because of new competition elsewhere and slowness in adjusting to changes in world trade. If MDCs want to grow faster, they can do so by investing in themselves, being dependent on LDCs only for relatively small investments in mining.

Another gain turns on the possibility that food may become scarce over the next two decades. This possibility could be reduced by investing more in agriculture (in the several ways that make up the agricultural package). One result would be a fall in the price of food. This would affect the relative incomes of farmers and non-farmers; it does not fit the distinction I am making between developed and developing countries. In the absence of an agricultural package (or if it were unsuccessful), MDCs would have to make food available for famine relief from their own production and stocks. It would be better to spend that money now and prevent the shortage.

There is a prima facie case that more-developed countries would benefit from development in less developed countries but we do not know what the orders of magnitude may be.

Discrimination in Employment · 4

THE RECENT FLOW of economic writing on discrimination was initiated by Gary Becker, who explored the consequences of assuming that either white employers or white employees disliked working with black persons. These assumptions led to the conclusion that black workers would earn less than white on the same job to compensate for this prejudice. However, this result would hold only if employers were unanimous in wanting such compensation. If not, some of them would hire only black workers and drive the discriminating firms out of the market. Various changes were rung on these themes, such as what would happen if all-black teams were not possible; if employers varied in their degree of prejudice, and so on. But the target that the book set itself—to explain how two people could be paid differently for doing the same job—dominated the field, not only in Becker's book but in most of the writing that followed.

Whatever the solution in short-term equilibrium, Becker's demonstration that discrimination could not occur in long-run competitive conditions is not only correct, but important to minority strategy. Under competitive pressure some employers will ignore color and drive their competitors out of business.

Another model that seeks to explain two prices for labor in the same market is that known as "statistical discrimination" originated by Edmund Phelps. Here the employer has no prejudice. He knows, however, that the average member of the minority group has less education and lower skills than the average member of the majority. He has the option of hiring a minority person who is applying for work or one belonging to the majority. The employer knows nothing about the minority individual, but he knows that the average member of the minority group has lower productivity and that if he chooses the minority person, he runs the chance of getting lower productivity. He will therefore not choose the minority person unless he is available at lower wages than the majority person. This establishes a difference of pay at the time of hiring. But after hiring a minority person at a lower wage, the employer will observe the employee's actual performance and may or may not adjust the wage accordingly, depending on the pressures to which he is subject.

In general, pressure for discrimination comes not from employers but from other employees. Its purpose, conscious or unconscious, is to preserve the more attractive jobs for those who are discriminating and to keep the remuneration of such jobs high by keeping the numbers eligible for them low. Also at stake are on-the-job training, promotion, and job security. Loss of employment hangs as a threat over the worker's head, with its consequence of losing his place in the skilled labor force and finding himself falling into the pool of cheap labor. The less competition there is for the desirable jobs, the less likely this is to happen. Malice is not a necessary ingredient of such attitudes; self-preservation is enough.

The model of the dual labor market, as developed by Peter Doerringer and Michael J. Piore is helpful to examining what is going on. Essentially, some workers get into the better jobs, while the rest get the mediocre jobs. At any given time (after training is completed) those with better jobs also have higher productivity, otherwise it would not pay the employers to support the dual labor market. The problem arises when we assume that at the moment of entering the market the two sets of employees have equal productivity and potential and that the higher productivity is acquired; for in competitive situations the lifetime value of one set of jobs would be no greater than the lifetime value of the other. Higher earnings in good jobs in middle and later life would be offset by lower value of good jobs at the beginning. This can be prevented only if entry to the good-jobs market is restricted, so that its premium cannot be competed away. The empirical task is to identify the barriers that maintain the dual system.

Discrimination need not turn on race. The exploited group could be women, or tall men, or foreigners. Two conditions determine the pattern. One is that the exploited group must have a lower supply price than the dominant group—otherwise both groups would earn the same. An unlimited supply of exploitable labor helps. The second condition is that the exploiters must have some cohesion—a sense of cohesion combined with some degree of righteousness. The cleavages most to be expected are those of race, ethnicity, and sex. Marx thought that cleavages must run horizontally, between capitalists and workers, but society has had many situations where the vertical cleavages are more powerful than the horizontal, such as the attitudes of white workers toward black workers in the southern states or of German workers toward guest workers in Germany.

Employers tend to go along with their employees on questions of group solidarity. They personally may lack prejudices, yet may be willing to discriminate. Such action is self-fulfilling. If members of subordinate groups are not hired for good jobs, or, if hired, do not receive the same on-the-job training as others or get the same opportunities to exercise responsibility, they will become less productive workers. Members of the dominant group can then discriminate against them with good conscience and a certainty of lack of malice, whereas in fact it is the lack of opportunity that has created the productive inferiority.

The technique is to reserve different jobs for different races, with the white jobs paying substantially more than the black jobs. Because, when allowance is made for training, the difference in wages exceeds the difference in productivity, the interests of employers and white trade unions diverge. The employers want to hire more blacks and fewer whites, and the unions want to protect the job by fixing its minimum wage at the level of the white. One of the problems of segregated societies is how to provide enough jobs for whites of less-than-average capability in the face of potential competition from some blacks of more-than-average capability but lower pay. Strong unions achieve this by reserving for whites an adequate number of jobs at white pay. Strong employers for their part reclassify jobs downward, turning what used to be a job for whites at higher pay into a job for blacks at lower pay. Depending upon the outcome, the job comes to be seen as a white job or as a black job; of, if segregation is breaking down, the job may even be open to both black and white at the white level of pay.

For black and white to perform the same job at different levels of pay also presupposes, besides a weak trade union, that the employer is not in sharp competition with another employer, each pressuring the other to trim his costs. This is the case in government service; and absence of competition explains why women teachers and clerks have for so long been paid less than their male counterparts. But even there males have tended to be eliminated from these "female" jobs.

Given the strength of union and competitive forces in private employment, one is not likely to find blacks and whites side by side doing exactly the same work at different levels of pay—at least not in the United States. What discrimination does is to preserve the better jobs for whites and relegate blacks (and white women) to the bottom of the labor market. This helps to keep up the wages of the better jobs, which are also those that have the lowest unemployment and the best promotion prospects.

A simple version is given in the appendix to this chapter. The question posed is whether employers benefit from discrimination or whether the gains of white workers are partly at their expense. The model uses the image of two separate islands, one occupied by blacks and the other by whites. No migration of labor is allowed at first (employers may move freely), and workers receive their marginal product, which is higher on the white than on the black island, because of superior fertility of their soil; the workers would have equal capacity on land of equal quality. At the next stage migration is opened up, and just enough workers migrate to make the marginal product of work the same on either island. Output increases because the marginal product of the workers who migrated is higher on the white island. White wages fall, black wages rise. Do the employers gain or lose from desegregation?

Employers fall into at least two groups. Those who employ whites are better off, because white wages have fallen; those who employ blacks are worse off, because black wages have risen; subject to the fact that total output has risen.

How about employers as a whole? The net result depends on three magnitudes: (1) On the size of the changes in wages as jobs are opened up to black labor; this depends on the elasticity of substitution between labor and other inputs. (2) On the relative numbers of blacks and whites who get higher or lower wages. (3) On the amount by which output increases as some blacks move into more productive jobs. So, the profits of employers as a whole—whether they have some interest in discrimination or not—may go up or down or be unchanged. But "employers as a whole" may not be a useful concept if much is at stake in the division between those who would benefit and those who would lose from desegregation.

Can employers retain gains from discrimination indefinitely? Are there long-run forces that hold profits at some norm, and which therefore redistribute abnormal profits toward higher wages or lower product prices? This depends on your theory of wages and profits.

Profits cannot be sustained indefinitely at exploitation level on the economists' conventional assumption that employers are competing with each other and will compete profits down to a level corresponding to the marginal product of capital. This assumes that the marginal product of capital is determined elsewhere in the economy, unaffected by discrimination, or even is determined outside the economy by an inflow and outflow of capital that keeps profits in the discrminating part of the economy tied to profits in capital markets elsewhere. This bears some resemblance to the United States.

This convention is debatable. Nobody has produced a theory of profits that provides universal satisfaction. In an alternative theory profits are a residual item. Wages are determined by the historical standard of living, which rises slowly. We may think of the supply curve of labor as more or less horizontal, but rising at, say, 2 percent a year. In this case the level of profits is not constrained by competition, and any benefits accruing to employers from discrimination will remain. This bears some resemblance to the determination of profits in India.

Employers as a group are most likely to favor going along with discrimination where the cost of paying blacks equally would be very high, either because the black wage would rise substantially with only a small or no fall in the white wage or else because of the relatively large number of blacks involved compared to whites. Under pressure the normal reaction is to open top jobs to blacks at white rates of pay, thereby discriminating among blacks: in other words, to pay the higher wage only to those blacks who are incorporated into the white job structure and not to blacks of equal competence who remain in the black part of the system. This is how the disintegration of segregated systems usually begins. White jobs near the top are opened up to blacks at white wages, but the gap between median white and median black wages is unaltered. Of course other blacks benefit indirectly, for the total number of jobs open to them is increased.

The success of this partial desegregation "strategy" depends somewhat on the black labor market. If one makes the extreme assumption of an unlimited supply of labor, then the migration of some blacks into white jobs does nothing for the blacks who remain in black jobs. Such an assumption would hardly apply to the United States, unless one reads in these terms the large outflow of women from the household into the labor market and also the flood of illegal immigrants. But it is probably a good vantage point for understanding the South African mining industry, which draws on labor from Southern and Central Africa. And it explains why desegregation would cost employers more in some situations than in others.

The essence of discrimination is its measures to restrict relative numbers in higher paid occupations. Race is not a necessary factor; such measures are found even in homogeneous societies. The big surge of trade unionism in the second half of the nineteenth century was among skilled workers, and many of their unions were concerned as much with limiting the numbers admitted to training as with wages and other conditions. We do not know all the factors that produced the caste system in India, but one of its results has been to hold down the numbers eligible for the more remunerative occupations, at the expense of those lower in the social scale.

The strategy is not confined to employees and trade unions, but is found also among the self-employed. Various professions use one device or another to restrict entry. Usually they defend their tests or other constraints in terms of benefits to the customer; nothing is said about the effect on the real incomes of the poor.

One must distinguish between intentional and consequential discrimination. Restricting the numbers eligible for the better jobs does not have racial or ethnic consequences in homogeneous societies; but in racial societies such measures have racial consequences because the persons most likely to be excluded, even by nonracial rules, will turn out to be members of the subordinate race. Moreover, the division increases with time; for those who are excluded do not get the same continuing learning opportunities as those who are included, nor do they pass the same enhanced cultural richness to the next generation. Consequential discrimination is then embedded in the system.

Legal approaches to discrimination go only part of the way. American law makes it illegal to pay different wages for the same work, though in competitive situations both the unions and the market would make this impractical anyway. The law then continues on to affirmative action, requiring firms to institute reasonable quotas in the higher-paying jobs. Eventually the law will consider legislation regarding the paying of different wages for different work of comparable worth. (A law dealing with this is still under consideration in the United States Congress.)

The most effective destroyer of discrimination is fast economic growth. This creates a shortage of skilled workers and incites employers to upgrade persons and jobs—unless white labor can be imported from abroad. Tightness in the labor market also reassures skilled workers, making them more willing to accept liberal policies.

APPENDIX:
THE GAIN TO EMPLOYERS FROM DISCRIMINATION

This figure illustrates the benefit or loss to employers, as a class, who discriminate between groups of workers assumed to be equally productive.

Suppose that there are two islands, one more fertile than the other. At the starting point whites only are employed on the more fertile island and blacks only on the less fertile island. Each worker is paid the marginal product of his group.

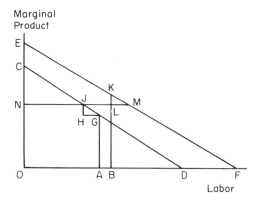

The marginal productivity of workers on the black island is given by *CD* and that of the white island by *EF*. Migration is not permitted. *EF* lies above *CD* because of superior fertility.

Suppose that there are *OA* workers on the black island. Their wage will be *AG*. Suppose that there are *OB* workers on the white island. Their wage will be *BK*.

Output is below the maximum. To transfer some men from the black to the white island would increase the total product.

Let this transfer be made, continuing to the point where marginal product is the same on both islands. (To preserve legibility the construction required for this is not shown in the diagram. It is as follows. Add *CD* and *EF* horizontally. The new line shows how many workers are employed if marginal product is the same on both islands. Find the point on this line that provides employment for all the workers, no more and no less.)

In the diagram the line *MLJN* makes the marginal products the same and provides jobs for all. *HG* persons have been transferred to the white island where they turn up as *LM*. Thus, $HG = LM$.

The employers' expenditure on black wages moves from $OA.GA$ to $ON.OA$. Note that $GA = (ON - HJ)$.

The employers' expenditure on white wages goes from $OB.BK$ to $ON.OB$. Note that $BK = (ON + KL)$.

Against these expenditures the employers can set the increased output, which is $0.5HG(KL + JH)$.

All together the increased expenditure on wages comes to:

$$(ON.OB + ON.OA) - (OB.ON + OB.KL)$$

$$- (OA.ON - OA.HJ)$$

$$= OA.HJ - OB.KL.$$

This result can be negative, positive, or zero, with or without the gain in output.

As the text indicates, the concept of a net gain or loss by employers as a whole is of limited value since some groups gain and others lose, and they do not necessarily act "as a whole."

Upward Mobility · 5

I HAVE ARGUED that inequality of black and white takes the form not so much of paying different prices for the same service as of reducing the opportunities for competition for the more highly remunerated jobs. This chapter and the next study the working of racial differentiation in the U.S. labor market. The extent of this differentiation can be measured. For example, in the year 1980 the median earnings of U.S. males, black and white together, was $13,994. The number of black males earning $13,994 or more was 1,780,000, equivalent to 31 percent. Equality would demand 50 percent above the median, so there was a deficit of 19 percent of jobs, or just about 1.1 million. Blacks had too few jobs above the median, and of course an equal number too many below the median.

Note that this measures not discrimination but distance from equality. Two groups may differ from each other in education, age, experience, or other factors. For the moment we are not explaining the differential; we are only measuring it.

We can make the same calculation for American women. The result is quite different. The median earnings of white women and black women are the same. The remuneration is low, but such as it is they compete for it on equal terms. However, the medians do not give the whole picture. If we take the number of persons earning more than $20,000 a year in 1980, this is 3.8 percent of black women earners and 4.9 percent of white women earners, indicating that although the medians are the same, white women are more successful than black women in competing for the best jobs.

However, this differentiation is very small when compared with the situation of men, where the proportion earning $20,000 or more is 33.4 percent. Women are a long way from economic equality with men. Median earnings for the United States as a whole (both sexes and both races) was $9,990. If this were to become the median for black women, there would be a deficit of about a million above-median jobs for black women. Taking men and women together, the black economy has a deficit of about two million above-median jobs and a corresponding surplus of two million below-median jobs.

A different form of measurement enables us to pinpoint the occupations where blacks have not yet caught up. If we take the percentage of blacks employed in any particular occupation (for example, 17.1 percent of black males are craftsmen) and the percentage of whites in that occupation, the difference between the two percentages gives us the deficit (or surplus) of black persons in that occupation. Thus, in 1980 the total deficit of black males in the occupations where they were in deficit was 21.5 percent (professional and technical, 5 percent; managerial, 8 percent; salesmen, 3 percent; craftsmen, 4 percent; farm managers, 2 percent). This is a deficiency of 1.2 million of the better kinds of jobs, and compares with the 1.1 million reached a moment ago by working with the medians.

The same calculation for black women, compared with all women, black and white, yields deficiencies in the same occupations. The black female deficit was 15.8 percent (professional, 2 percent; managerial, 3 percent; saleswomen, 4 percent; clerical, 6 percent; crafts, 0.4 percent). This comes to 985,000. The deficits at the sales level and the clerical level are specially notable. Surely they would respond to treatment.

These calculations are not watertight, but the conclusion that blacks in the United States are short of about two million above-median jobs seems inescapable. Another point brought out by the calculations is that, even for men, the big deficiency is in white-collar jobs (16 percent) rather than in blue-collar jobs (4 percent). The figures cannot be taken as precise, for a breakdown into a greater number of occupations might yield more blue-collar categories where blacks are in deficit and more white-collar categories where whites are in deficit; but the results of such a breakdown would differ only marginally.

Corresponding to this deficit of above-median jobs is a surplus of the same number of below-median jobs. This surplus could be close to the median, but it is not. A large part of it is at the very bottom of the scale. To raise the earnings of blacks at the bottom would not effect the difference between black and white median earnings, but it would raise the mean of black incomes and so approach nearer to economic equality. It would also of course strike at the very heart of poverty.

If economic equality is to be attained, the task defines itself as follows. First, to raise the earnings of blacks performing jobs at the bottom of the scale. And second, to find more above-median jobs for blacks, whether by promotion in their existing occupations or by opening up new occupations. These two tasks are related, for the removal of two million people from below- to above-median jobs would take some pressure off the labor supply in the poor-jobs market and so help to raise earnings there. The tension sometimes found between people who are trying to open up more above-median jobs and those who are working on earnings lower down the scale results from a misunderstanding of mutual concerns.

Where are two million above-median jobs to be found for blacks? This is not an easy task, but it is not as formidable as it sounds on first hearing. Because the black labor force is only about 10 percent of the whole, rather large adjustments in its structure require only minor adjustments on the part of the rest of the nation. Thus, in 1980 the number of above-median jobs was about fifty-three million, of which two million is only 3.8 percent. Nevertheless, the deficiency cannot be eliminated in one year. It involves more vocational and technical education for blacks, more on-the-job training, and that accretion of experience which in the passage of time qualifies for the highest appointments. If the current rates of change continue, they will eliminate half of the deficiency over the next ten years, but the last half will take longer. The program also demands more cooperation on the part of white Americans, which is more likely to be achieved if the economy is expanding rapidly and creating many more good jobs than if depression continues.

Those at the bottom of the labor market have been under great pressure during the past two or three decades because of trends in supply and demand that have been working against them.

On the side of supply, the vast influx of women into the labor market has affected bottom jobs most, since women fill such jobs disproportionately. Also augmenting the supply of cheap labor in the United States has been the immigration of Puerto Ricans to the mainland, of Mexicans, documented and undocumented, and of other Hispanics. Competition between Hispanics and blacks is sharper on the Eastern seaboard; it seems more muted on the West coast, but only because the black population there is still relatively small. However, the black population there is growing rapidly; in California it increased at 4 percent per year between 1960 and 1975, when it reached 8 percent of the state's population. The black population is bound to be affected by what happens to the inflow of Mexicans, especially as this group moves from agriculture into urban occupations.

On the side of demand, changes in agricultural technology have nearly eliminated the demand for farm workers, whose share of black employment fell from 14.5 percent in 1955 to 2 percent in 1980, an elimination of about a million jobs. These were also decades in which the mechanization of service jobs proceeded rapidly, helped to some extent by a sharp and continuing relative fall in the price of oil. Jobs in laundries, kitchens, and the cleaning of offices and houses gave way to domestic appliances. The spread of self-service in restaurants, hotels, shops, and elsewhere had the same effect on employment.

The situation is not revealed by looking at statistics of the total number of people employed. Jobs increased in number as fast as the numbers seeking work, but the number of mediocre jobs was disproportionately large. Using Bureau of Labor statistics, Bennett Harrison and Barry Bluestone write: "Since the late 1960s some 67 percent of all new jobs in the United States have been in industries that paid average annual wages and salaries of less than $13,600 (in 1980 dollars). In 1969 only 45 percent of all jobs were in that category" (*The New York Times*, June 19, 1984).

This oversupply at the bottom of the labor market, which goes back to the late 1950s, contrasts with the situation in other Western economies. Their demand for skilled labor, especially in manufacturing and construction, was growing more rapidly than American demand. It was met by training and upgrading workers into the skilled trades, while replacing them in lower-paid jobs with immigrants from Southern Europe and the Mediterranean countries.

Two of the factors affecting unskilled labor negatively in the 1950s and 1960s should have less influence in the future. One is the decline of the agricultural labor force, which swelled the supply of unskilled labor for urban occupations. The other is that oil is no longer cheap and the mechanization of unskilled jobs is marginally less attractive. But women will continue to pour into the market for at least another decade,

Hispanics will continue to arrive, and the outlook for general economic expansion is even more clouded.

There are three ways to increase the earnings of unskilled labor: raise its productivity; fix its price; and reduce the supply.

Other things being equal, increased productivity in a single industry will raise the demand for labor—if the demand for its product has the right degree of elasticity. The mechanization of agriculture in the 1950s and the 1960s weakened the position of unskilled labor, as did (it seems probable) mechanization in some of the service jobs. Besides, other things are *not* equal when mechanization is occurring everywhere. What happens to employment, then, depends on whether investment is growing fast enough to take up the labor slack. Despite predictions to the contrary, over the last century and a half mechanization has presented the business community with enough new opportunities for investment not only to offset technological unemployment but also to absorb the expansion of the labor force through births and immigration. As David Ricardo argued, technology will not outrun employment if the extra profits and savings stimulate enough new investment. But the investment ratio in the United States was rather low in the 1960s, by comparison with other developed countries, and it was lower still in the 1970s.

Minimum wages may be set by governmental machinery, or by collective bargaining, or indirectly by fixing unemployment compensation or welfare payments at levels that raise the supply curve of labor. Where wages have been very low, to fix a minimum almost certainly pays for itself by increasing the worker's strength and alertness. Beyond this, it may reduce the demand for labor, by how much we do not know. But it seems not inappropriate for a rich country to fix a minimum wage and to meet through its social security system any unemployment which this may cause. It is to the credit of Marxist-inspired societies that the abolition of absolute poverty is among their first priorities, and there is no reason why rich capitalist societies, inspired by religious ideals, should lag in this respect.

The principal target for the black community should be to reduce the number of young people seeking work as unskilled laborers, by providing them with the opportunity to acquire, if they so desire, credentials and skills that make them eligible for better-paid jobs. If the children of those who now work at the bottom were eligible for jobs farther up the scale, they would not seek the same jobs as their parents and could be hired for such jobs only if pay scales were raised to comparability with their new eligibilities. For full effectiveness, this requires also the opening up of more above-median jobs. To help those at the bottom, one must move some of the bottom into the middle and some of the middle into the top; operation at the various levels of black employment is not competitive but complementary.

Assuming for the moment that young blacks do acquire the relevant skills, there remain obstacles to their getting better-paid jobs. One of these obstacles to entry is action on the part of trade unions or other groups aimed at denying employment to blacks in specific jobs. Such action is now illegal and, under the influence of responsible trade union leaders, is much less pervasive than it used to be. But the leaders are ahead of the rank and file, and not all leaders are effectively in line. So the situation requires continual monitoring and pressure.

The second obstacle to getting into the better jobs is the need to pass tests which are irrelevant, culture-bound, or even designed to trap black candidates. This obstacle is more difficult to pin down. The black community cannot object to relevant and fair tests, since it, too, will be dependent on quality service from those who pass the tests, and it, too, is inspired by ideals of efficiency and excellence. None of this, however, supports testing that is irrelevant or unfair.

A third obstacle is the need, when applying for a position, to be personally recommended by someone whose recommendation carries weight. When the firm's employees are the chief recommenders and nearly all these employees are white, this can be a formidable barrier, even without malice. Because personal recommendation is a major element in hiring at all job levels, right up to top managerial and professional posts, it is one of the main obstacles to the employment of blacks. One can conclude that blacks need to increase their contacts with whites in all possible ways; social and other segregation is harmful to the effort to break into better jobs. Another possible remedy is to work harder at personal recommendation. The National Urban League already runs a placement service for highly skilled occupations. It, or some other civil rights organization, should consider extending such a service widely— for example, by attaching counselors to every high school or community college to sponsor graduates of above-median quality. This would be a formidable task, even if maintained largely by volunteers (black and white), and the service would have to be built up gradually.

The fourth obstacle to blacks' obtaining better jobs is the need to finance a learning period in one's first job. In some jobs the worker starts on probation at a low wage and may spend as much as a year or more being trained in the work he will do, after which his salary increases rapidly. Middle-class parents help their children to finance this learning period, but many working-class parents who would like to help cannot afford it and are discouraged by the opportunities their children have to pass by.

Similar obstacles also stand in the way of promotion within the firm after one has secured employment. Promotion may require prior selection for training courses, which can be blocked by the hostility of other employees, by irrelevant tests, or by the absence of recommendation. Lack of seniority can be a problem, especially in firms or insititutions where seniority rights are guarded by unions and governed by industrial agreements.

As we saw in Chapter 2, affirmative action is an appropriate way, in theory, to deal with these obstacles to employment and promotion to better jobs. But it is not practicable to prescribe how many minority persons each of scores of thousands of firms must hire in various categories over the next five years. Past progress in this area has come from direct action by the civil rights movement, from boycotting firms with unfair employment practices, from lying down in the road in front of building contractors' vehicles, and from other such direct tactics. Direct action and liberal support have led to equal employment opportunity laws, with commissions to enforce them, at federal, state, and local levels. Enforcement is uneven because resources allocated for this purpose are meager. This is an opportunity not adequately exploited.

Close contact with white trade union leaders is necessary, because unions effectively control recruitment and promotion over wide areas. They control apprenticeship programs and much else. Top union leadership has moved in the right direction, even if it has not always been able to control the rank and file. Black leaders and union leaders should meet more often and contribute more to each other's deliberations.

We have an index of black progress in blue-collar jobs, namely, the proportion of blacks in "craft and kindred" trades. This group of workers has survived all the forces leading to a reduction of the proportion of blue-collar workers in the labor force. Indeed, the percentage of craft and kindred in all male employment (black and white) rose from 15 percent in 1940 to 20 percent in 1960 and 1970, and 21 percent in 1980. Of these totals, the black share was 2.3 percent in 1940, 4.2 percent in 1960, 5.5 perecent in 1970, and 8.2 percent in 1980 (when 10 percent would represent equal participation). So blacks have been gaining steadily where it matters, even during the depressed 1970s.

It is important for young blacks with working-class backgrounds and aspirations to realize that some blacks have managed to penetrate these desirable craft occupations, and that the proportion is steadily growing. The temptation to deny that it is happening should be resisted. For some part of the failure of black achievement is attributable to low horizons while in school or just out of school. There is good reason for blacks to have low horizons, because of all that has been experienced in opportunities denied and, especially at this time, because of very heavy juvenile unemployment. It is not possible to say how much of the problem originates here. Even if a substantial minority of young blacks is discouraged, a very substantial proportion is alert and ready to seize any opportunity, and this number exceeds the number of better-paid blue-collar jobs available to young blacks. So we have not yet reached the point where a lack of suitable candidates can explain the deficit of blacks in such jobs. If we could find enough good openings for all who qualify, horizons would extend rapidly and this part of the problem would disappear.

The largest deficit of better-paid jobs for blacks is in white-collar occupations. The deficit exists at all levels: it is relatively greatest at the highest levels, but the absolute numbers involved are largest at the lowest levels.

White-collar occupations grow in numbers faster than blue-collar occupations. Taking all races together, white-collar occupations made up 32 percent of the jobs in 1940, 41 percent in 1960, 46 percent in 1970, and 52 percent in 1980.

Blacks have made big gains in the white-collar occupations too, though they are still lagging. In 1980 only 39 percent of employed blacks were in white-collar occupations, compared with 54 percent of whites. But the black share of these occupations had risen from 1.9 percent in 1940, to 3 percent in 1960, 5 percent in 1970, and 6.6 percent in 1980. The statistics are treacherous; definitions have changed and the ratios are cyclical; but the upward trend is unmistakable.

The position of women differs from that of men in that the difference of earnings between the races is greater for men than for women. One can trace the relative improvement of the situation of black women by looking at the data for persons in the highest occupations (professional, technical, managerial, and administrative) who in 1980 were 27 percent of the labor force (all races, both sexes). The percentage shares of each subdivision by race and sex employed in this group of occupations are shown in the accompanying table.

Group	1940	1960	1970	1980
White men	17	23	26	31
Black men	3	5	8	17
White women	19	18	19	24
Black women	5	8	11	19

It is clear that black women have gained on white women very substantially, while still having some distance to go. White and black female median earnings (for full-time work) may be the same outside the South, but upper-quartile earnings are not. We can also see that black women have advanced further in these occupations than black men, though not as far as white men. What pulls the median for black women below the median for black men is the disproportionately large number of black females in the lowest-paid service occupations. The target for black female employment is to get out of these service trades into sales and clerical occupations and into the professional and administrative categories.

Opposition to the employment of well-qualified blacks is less organized in white-collar than in blue-collar occupations because of the weakness of trade unions there. But most occupations share some of the same problems, especially the need to be recommended, the financing of a learning period, and obstacles in the way of promotion. Blacks are also excluded from some jobs requiring face-to-face contact with the customer (such as sales jobs, receptionists, and some professional jobs) if the employer thinks that some customers might be offended at having to deal with blacks. Part of this problem is the unfavorable image of blacks in the minds of white persons, one which, like the unfavorable image of whites in the minds of black persons, will take at least two more generations to eradicate.

Image apart, black young people need better preparation if they are to get and hold 10 percent of white-collar jobs. Above all, a much higher proportion must complete high school; the report that 45 percent of students drop out of high school in New York City is appalling. Also, those who complete high school deserve a better education; too often the curriculum is deficient, even in teaching the three R's. In addition, the atmosphere does not prepare the student for the workaday world in which he will have to live. Employers expect discipline, punctuality, responsibility, respectful behavior, the carrying out of instructions, and the absence of physical violence. Middle-class white children are taught such things in their schools and homes; but a large proportion of black children are in schools whose effect is to make them less well prepared for the work place rather than better prepared. Thus, the unfortunate image of black youth acquires some substance.

It must be recognized that our objective—to raise a substantial fraction of a group from working class to middle class—is inconsistent with the hierarchial nature of societies and the means by which they maintain stable structures. Despite all the talk of social mobility, the open door, and equality of opportunity, the main effect of schooling on class structure has been to retain middle-class jobs for middle-class children, since middle-class parents are better than working-class parents at getting their children through schooling and past the usual tests. So, too, the need for recommendation when seeking jobs aids those who mingle with persons in authority and have friends who can get them a hearing. Blacks have, therefore, not one barrier but two: color and class.

The question of image is difficult for blacks because of the feeling that an ethnic minority is entitled to be different. This is beyond question. But different in what ways? The question takes us back to the discussion of interracial goals. Human beings are alike in most respects; what differences does one wish to establish or preserve? The answer is usually given in terms of culture (music, literature, painting), social relations (extended family relations, political authority), religion, and customs (ceremonies, parties, food).

One potential difference is for the ethnic minority to be poorer than the rest of the society. This difference has been rejected by ethnic white minorities in the United States, to the point that some of them (for example, Jews, Irish) have higher average incomes than the rest of the white population. This result is achieved by adopting competitive efficiency as a test of what differences may be retained and rejecting differences that make the group less competitive. Accordingly, these groups send their children to disciplined schools, ensure that they are fluent in English (whether as a first or as a second language), and emphasize the goal of doing as well at school as one's abilities permit. If blacks wish to achieve racial economic equality, they, too, must use competitive efficiency as a test of what differences to maintain.

Poor schooling underlies the low status of blacks in the labor market. This deficiency has been inflicted deliberately on this racial group by those who have controlled the schools. Its cumulative effects are not easily reversed. For white ethnic minorities, schools have been an avenue of advancement and schooling at the center of community concerns. But in the eyes of many black children, schooling has led nowhere; indeed, until recently those who finished high school earned no more than those who dropped out two or three years earlier. If the schools improve their usefulness, they will come to be cherished, discipline will be restored, standards will rise, and they will be even more useful, in a cumulative progression. Good schooling would transform the black situation in the United States.

Unemployment · 6

IN THE UNITED STATES as whole unemployment is higher now than it averaged in the 1950s and 1960s. In 1980 unemployment averaged 12.3 and 6.1 percent for black and white men respectively, and 13.1 and 6.5 for black and white women respectively. These differentials have been more or less constant throughout the postwar period, unlike those of teenage unemployment, which have been increasing. We shall deal first with adult unemployment, and consider teenage unemployment separately.

Why is the adult black unemployment ratio persistently about twice as high as the white? The answers fall into two categories: relatively more blacks than whites work in the industries and occupations that are most subject to unemployment; and blacks are more subject to unemployment than whites in the same jobs.

Blacks are more subject to unemployment in all industries and occupations, so the second category of explanations is the more important. However, it is also true that unemployment is lower in white-collar than in blue-collar occupations (3.7 and 10.0 percent). In each case blacks have five percentage points more unemployment than whites, but the fact that the proportion of white-collar workers is higher for whites than for blacks itself reduces the white ratio.

One reason for higher unemployment in blue-collar occupations is the tradition of the labor market. In the past blue-collar workers were understood to be employed on a daily basis, while white-collar workers, domestic servants, and farm laborers were on tenure for life. Blue-collar workers have had to fight hard to get such job security as they now have. A large percentage of blue-collar work is still on short contract (daily, weekly, monthly). Labor turnover in these jobs is high, and considerable time elapses between jobs, sometimes voluntarily, since habit and welfare payments together breed a certain taste for between-work vacations. Why is more blue-collar work not on tenure? I suggest that the answer is tradition, bearing in mind the Japanese tradition of lifetime tenure for a large proportion of blue-collar workers. The principle reason may be that the white-collar worker acquires knowledge about the business of his firm that is useful to his employer and justifies keeping him through periods of slack. But the differences are only of degree.

The main reason for higher unemployment in blue-collar than white-collar occupations is that, ever since the 1950s, the market for unskilled labor has been overcrowded. As we saw, a combination of mechanization, agriculture's expulsion of labor, the influx of women into the labor market, illegal immigration, and the slow growth of the economy kept supply running ahead of demand in the market for unskilled labor. Wages have risen fast almost certainly faster than productivity in the low-wage service trades, so it is easy to understand the persistent imbalance between supply and demand for unskilled labor. The remedy is to reduce the supply of unskilled labor by imparting more skills and to effect faster growth of the economy.

Yet another cause of higher blue-collar and low-wage service-industry unemployment is the residual role of this market in relation to other labor markets. Wages are fixed at all levels of earnings and tend to be inflexible in relation to each other. Any excess of supply in the well-paid trades creates unemployment there, and the displaced tend to move downward in search of work. So disequilibrium at the top shows itself eventually not in unemployment at the top but in pressure on wages at the bottom, with perhaps also unemployment at the bottom. In reverse, in times of prosperity the upper grades take on more labor, and there is less pressure on wages at the bottom as well as less unemployment there. The overcrowding of the market for unskilled labor ever since the 1950s reflects the failure of the upper grades to expand their absorption fast enough to cope with the overall growth of the labor force. One small index of this is that the ratio of the median wage of white women fully at work to that of white men fell steadily from 63 percent in 1956 to 57 percent in 1974—though a widening of the differential is not an essential part of the process.

Why is unemployment greater among blacks than among whites in the same occupations and industries? The first answer is cyclical: blacks are the last to be hired and the first to be fired. Pressure on and through trade unions has tended to reduce this in organized trades, but union insistence on the rights of seniority also works in the opposite direction. This phenomenon shows up markedly in the statistics. Black unemployment rises swiftly in the early states of recession, but more slowly in the later stages. If white unemployment is less than 4 percent, black unemployment rises by about two and a half to three percentage points for each one percentage point rise in white unemployment; but above 5 percent white unemployment the ratio falls to about 1.5 to 1.0. Race prejudice of course plays a role, as management decides whom to lay off and whom to keep. But it is also possible that some of the blacks who are last hired are also marginally the least productive.

The gap in unemployment percentages is not, however, a cyclical phenomenon; it persists at all stages of the cycle. One explanation is thought to be the emigration of industry from city centers to suburbs. The housing built in these suburbs tends to be occupied mainly by whites—either because it is expensive or because of illegal but effective methods of exclusion. Black workers own relatively few automobiles. So it is expensive for black central-city residents to go to the suburbs in search of jobs, and if they get such jobs the cost of travel, both in money and in mental and physical exhaustion, is exorbitant.

This line of reasoning leads to two alternative possible policies for matching jobs and homes. One is to assist blacks in moving to the suburbs where the new industries are. This is not easy, given the hostility of suburban residents and their power to manipulate zoning regulations. Nor is it popular with black political leaders, who argue that the political power of blacks derives from their living together and would be eroded if they scattered into the suburbs. They query whether the black unemployment ratios in the center and the suburbs are all that different, a question that can be answered appropriately only in conditions of moderate prosperity or better.

The other policy is to revivify central cities, to the point that industry would return. One special aspect of this would be the creation of new industry either within the area now largely black or just on its outskirts. Development corporations have indeed been created with this mandate. They have had some success—and all success is welcome—but one must not exaggerate what is possible. These areas became unattractive to their black residents as they became overcrowded and fell victim to crime, drugs, and poor sanitation. Black businesses were burglarized, ceased to get insurance, and closed. As middle-class residents moved away, conditions deteriorated, houses ceased to be repaired, and property was abandoned, vandalized, and burned. It is true that these forces are cumulative, and that if one could turn the situation around, the cumulative forces would work for a return to vitality and for prosperity. But it is not easy to turn such forces around. Development corporations that have succeeded in introducing industry have combined extraordinary diligence with excellent political and financial connections. Such fortuitous conjunctions should always be cherished and supported, but they will not provide the whole solution to the problem.

This line of reasoning has come under attack. It implies that employers move to the suburbs indifferent to the fact that they are leaving part of their labor force behind. Either that, or they do not need those whom they are leaving behind. In this case the problem is really that there is an overall surplus of labor, concentrated among blacks living in central cities. If this is the problem, it cannot be solved by moving blacks to the suburbs or industry to the center. Either of these policies might equalize the black and white unemployment rates, but would still leave a general surplus of labor. If, instead, one increased the overall demand for labor, industry presumably would find some way of bringing its plant and its labor force together.

Regional slackness is as important as general slackness. Industry has been migrating from the Northeast to the South and West, leaving behind the less mobile members of the population. Conceivably this affects black unemployment more than white.

Whatever the effect on unemployment, the case for rebuilding central areas and attracting business stands on its own feet once one recognizes that for one reason or another it is not going to be feasible to shift several hundred thousand blacks into the suburbs. One must build where the people are. This seems to be generally recognized, and many organizations promote the idea, but federal funding is slow and small.

Three explanations of why the black unemployment rate exceeds the white rate may add up to a sufficient answer. First, some jobs are more prone to unemployment than others, and a disproportionate number of blacks hold such jobs. Attention has been drawn to the difference between blue-collar jobs and white-collar jobs, but within these categories blacks hold the lower and marginal jobs that are equally prone to unemployment, whether held by blacks or whites. The withholding of promotion is especially relevant here. Temporary setbacks include the loss of a million farm jobs and the increase of the female labor force at a rate that cannot be sustained indefinitely (3.7 percent per year). These were traumatic events.

Second, once unemployed, blacks find it harder to get new jobs because of the need for personal recommendation when seeking a job. I have already mentioned this as one reason why blacks do not get their share of the better jobs. It also contributes to their being the last to be hired. I have suggested a placement service.

Finally, it is possible that there are marginally more blacks than whites at the lowest levels of industrial productivity and preparedness for employment—so that even at the top of a boom the economic system can find jobs for 97 percent of whites but only for 94 percent of blacks. (The difference is marginal, but it is vital to those immediately affected by a lack of work.) The number of years spent in school is sometimes taken as an index of preparedness for employment. Some 12 percent of black adults, compared with less than 3 percent of white adults, have spent fewer than five years in school. This is not just a matter of the benefits of schooling. Families that do not send their children to school tend also to be careless of their upbringing in other ways. So it is not surprising if in later life some adults with poor educational backgrounds or other deficiencies in upbringing cannot earn the minimum wage and therefore turn up in the unemployment statistics.

The impact of unpreparedness on unemployment is affected by the level of the minimum wage. Given the wage, the ultimate remedy is to invest more in the bodies and minds of the children of the poor, thereby reducing unemployables to the barest minimum. This involves the whole social program—

schools, health services, water supplies, housing, and so on. Such programs have been effective for white American children and for West European children, and would be equally effective with black American children. The United States is the only modern country that still has a lumpenproletariat.

When we turn to youth unemployment, we are in a different world, where the orders of magnitude are extraordinary. In 1977, for males aged sixteen to nineteen years, it averaged 16.2 percent for whites and 34.9 percent for blacks. And whereas the rate for whites has kept steady (though high) over twenty years, the rate for blacks has been rising most of the time. After we examine what black and white teenagers have in common that produces such high rates, we shall consider the additional factors that make the black rate higher still.

Owing to the relatively high birth rates of the 1950s and first part of the 1960s, the proportion of the population aged sixteen to nineteen has been abnormally high in the second half of the 1960s and in the 1970s. Between 1955 and 1977 this proportion rose from 7.6 to 10.5 percent of the adult population. Between 1955 and 1970 the increase in absolute numbers of sixteen- to nineteen-year-olds was at a rate of 3.7 percent per annum.

It has been suggested that one of the prime causes of high teenage unemployment is that the economy is not structured to employ such a high ratio of teenagers or to cope with such a rapid rate of growth in their numbers. The argument presupposes that teenagers have special employment characteristics, otherwise the numbers involved are too small to be a problem. At the height of the flood, the annual increase of this age group in the labor force was 267,000, which should have been absorbable into a labor force of 79 million without much difficulty.

The special employment characteristic of teenagers is lack of work experience. They have physical strength, and as much book learning as twenty-five-year-olds, whose unemployment ratio is much lower. Plant and equipment can be provided for them. The argument therefore narrows down to saying that firms can make use of only a limited number of inexperienced persons. Some trades that provide for apprenticeship do indeed limit the ratio of apprentices to journeymen; but this is a rather small part of the labor market. Otherwise, the argument merges into the discussion of the effects of the minimum wage, and can be translated into saying that firms can use only a limited number of inexperienced persons at the minimum wage.

The flood has subsided. The annual increase in this age group has been reduced to less than 50,000; soon it will be negative. The *shortage* of teenagers may be a talking point of the 1990s.

The minimum-wage argument turns on the proposition that for the same pay an employer will prefer an experienced adult worker to a teenager. At the height of a boom, when adults are not available, he will hire teenagers; but as the market slackens, he will choose adults in preference to teenagers. The argument need not state that the minimum wage exceeds the teenager's marginal product; it depends only on the absence of a pay differential corresponding with an experience differential.

In this form the argument seems unassailable. But unions are adamant against differentials for youth, arguing that this would merely redistribute unemployment, creating jobs for the young at the expense of jobs for their fathers. It would therefore take a period of prolonged prosperity to create an atmosphere in which such a reform could be made.

The "experience" to which I keep referring is only partly a matter of technical skills. It is also a matter of fitting into the culture patterns of factory and office life, which is more hierarchical, disciplined, and controlled than family life or life in school. The gap between the permissive life of home and school and the hierarchical life of the workplace has widened enormously over the past two decades, making it difficult for many young people to fit into economic life. Many wander in and out of jobs until about their middle twenties, when they finally settle down. While they are on their travels their children are maintained by the welfare system, which takes care of women with dependent children. To some observers the welfare system is at the core of the unemployment rate, since it makes it feasible for workers to be more choosy in the kinds of low-level jobs that they are willing to take and so raises the supply curve of teenage labor.

In most other parts of the world education is aimed specifically at preparing the young for the social patterns of their adult lives. It is odd that the United States should maintain a system of public schools whose permissive mores are so much at odds with what the young will have to adjust to at the workplace. Presumably, this anomaly cannot continue indefinitely, but it seems likely to last a long time.

Meanwhile much thought has been given to ways of easing the transition from school to work. These include spending a day or two per week at work while still in school, more summer vacation jobs for fifteen-year-olds, more training-type jobs on leaving school of the kind originally contemplated by the Comprehensive Employment and Training Act (CETA).

Teenage unemployment is not specifically an American problem; it is worldwide. It is best documented in the member countries of the Organization for Economic Cooperation and Development (OECD), where only Germany, Austria, and Switzerland have successfully alleviated it. To quote a 1981 OECD report (Shirley Williams et al., *Youth Without Work*): "The youth unemployment ratio exceeded that of adults by a factor of about two in Canada, Finland and Japan; by a factor of about three in Australia, France, Sweden, the United Kingdom and the United States; by more than four in Portugal and Spain; and by more than six in Italy. Yet Germany has succeeded in keeping youth unemployment at a rate close to that of adults" (page 94).

What accounts for this remarkable phenomenon in Germany? A combination of compulsory vocational training and compulsory apprenticeship. The same report states: "Young Germans must by law attend vocational achools for a minimum of eight hours a week after they leave school and until they reach the age of 18. The overwhelming majority of school leavers, over 90 percent, also enter into an apprenticeship, which is an individual contract with an employer intended to provide on the job training in a given occupation. The young person has to qualify by taking a series of tests and examinations" (page 16).

There are special features in the German situation: the acceptance of compulsion by the school leavers; the willingness of industry to provide so many apprenticeships in so many different fields; and the concurrence of the trade unions in a system where apprentices earn so much less than the adult minimum wage. Not least important has been the maintenance of full employment, which makes the special features possible. In fact as German unemployment has mounted in the 1980s, teenage unemployment has risen disproportionately. But the system is valuable even if it is not wholly resistant to big recessions. Its usefulness in moderate or prosperous economic conditions is still to be prized.

Why is the black teenage unemployment ratio so much higher than the white? What I have said about adults applies here also. First, some jobs are more prone to unemployment than others, and blacks are disproportionately in such jobs. Second, blacks, even when they are well-qualified and competent, have more difficulty in finding jobs, because they do not have the appropriate contacts; this, too, pushes them into the less-attractive jobs.

And finally, there is a large proportion of blacks whose preparation for employment is inadequate. They may come from less than adequate schools or have dropped out at an early age. There is quite a gap between the life style of teenagers, black or white, still in school and that of persons in the workplace, and the average gap is wider with blacks than with whites. The breakdown of the American public school system is particularly hard on blacks, since they depend on it disproportionately. At the same time, employers, having more candidates among whom to select, have raised their qualifications and are demanding to see more diplomas or certificates. This "credentialism" is an additional barrier to the employment of young people who have failed to complete their schooling.

The fact that white teenage unemployment is so high is the final reason why the black rate is astronomical. The market exerts no pressure on white business to hire blacks when the supply of whites is so enormous. One cannot make a substantial dent on the black rate unless the white rate is also significantly reduced. This turns on three changes that are hard to effect: a minimum-wage differential for experience; reform of the public schools; and full employment.

The state of the labor market in the United States affects the ways in which various groups fare. The American economy has been in a major recession since 1974, but its troubles go back earlier—to at least the 1950s. The situation is easily summarized by contrast with Western Europe. During the 1950s and 1960s the countries of Western Europe grew so rapidly that they ran short of labor. The bottleneck showed not in skilled but in unskilled labor; for as skilled workers became scarce, employers merely trained more unskilled workers and upgraded them. Many unskilled jobs were mechanized or abolished (by adopting self-service patterns). For the rest, unskilled labor was imported from the less prosperous Mediterranean countries and elsewhere.

The point at issue in comparing the American and European labor markets is not the total number of jobs provided, but the number of good jobs in contrast with mediocre jobs. U.S. employment grew as fast as the U.S. labor force. Unemployment ratios were low in the 1950s and 1960s, but it was the mediocre jobs that were taking up the slack.

The American economy needed to grow faster than the European economies, partly because its labor force was growing faster and also because its reservoirs of marginal labor were relatively larger. Instead, industrial production grew more slowly in the United States than in Western Europe: by 5.9 percent per annum in France, 5.5 percent in Germany, and 4.6 percent in the United States (counting from peak to peak, 1956 to 1969, centered on three-year averages). Industrial productivity grew faster than ever before over the past century, but the numbers employed advanced slowly.

In fact, industrial production grew so slowly in the United States that the numbers employed in manufacturing declined steadily as a percentage of the labor force; this phenomenon is now known as "deindustrialization." Between 1956 and 1969 numbers in manufacturing grew at 1.2 percent per annum, while the labor force grew at 1.5 percent per annum. It is true that some highly paid service sectors grew rapidly—finance and television, for example—but this growth, was not sufficient to create an excess demand for skills.

Deindustrialization is incompatible with the goals of the black population. If the economy is growing so slowly, its reservoirs of cheap labor fill up. People either become unemployed or find themselves in a disproportionate number of marginal jobs. Employment in manufacturing and other high-value sectors must grow over the next decade or two at least one percentage point faster than the labor force: say, at 2.5 when the labor force is growing at 1.5 percent per annum. If this occurs, then the expansion of skilled and better-paid jobs will decrease the reservoir of cheap labor, facilitating the upgrading that is our objective. This is impossible if manufacturing is not at least holding its share of employment.

Deindustrialization is sometimes attributed to the affluence of Americans, which brings a low elasticity of demand for manufactures vis-à-vis services. If this were the case, it would show up in low domestic utilization of manufactures (production plus imports minus exports). But this was not the case. Utilization was well maintained by the rapid inflow of imports. During the 1960s production of manufactures increased at 4.6 percent per annum, imports at 13 percent, and exports at 6 percent. According to the United Nations Conference on Trade and Development (UNCTAD), between 1959–60 and

1973–74 the share of imports in U.S. consumption of manufactures rose by five percentage points; this was exceeded only
by the United Kingdom, whose imports share rose by six percentage points. Both countries dwarfed the European Economic Community (EEC) and Japan, with two and one percentage points respectively. The United States was not
rejecting manufactures; it was importing them to an unusual
degree—a doubling every six years—instead of producing for
its own use.

The result of this bombardment by imports was that industry was relatively unprofitable. The United States investment
ratio was near the bottom of the list of OECD countries, its
growth rate among the slowest. Instead of the reservoir of
cheap labor emptying, as in continental Europe, it was filling.

All these phenomena are reminiscent of the British situation
in the last quarter of the nineteenth century. There, too, imports of manufactures rose faster than exports; domestic capital formation was low; and the growth rate was low. Very
large numbers continued to emigrate long after emigration
from Germany had reduced to a trickle.

Britain could survive because its large invisible income
from shipping, insurance, interest, and dividends mounted
swiftly. The United States balanced its payments in the 1960s
with mounting interest and dividends from abroad. For a
country to be in a balance of payments equilibrium and nevertheless be in disequilibrium at home, in terms of slow growth
and high unemployment, is now a widespread phenomenon
as familiar to us as its opposite. British historians disagree as
to whether the British case was a simple example of an overvalued exchange rate or reflected a more fundamental failure of
the British economy to make for itself an adequate place in the
new world economy of the second industrial revolution
(based on steel, electricity, the internal combustion engine,
and organic chemicals). American economists debate the case
of the United States in similar terms.

Whatever the basic nature of the American case, President
Nixon seized the initiative in 1971 by devaluing the dollar.

American industry was therefore given the opportunity to reverse the adverse conditions of the 1960s—to produce more and sell more both at home and abroad.

Just two years later however, industry was faced with a new setback: the great recession that started at the end of 1973. This is of course a disaster for the whole labor movement, black or white. But it is particularly disastrous for the attainment of economic equality between black and white. Equality requires that jobs above the median grow by about one percentage point faster than the labor force. Without some such upward thrust, attempts to move toward equalization face strong opposition and bitterness. Economic growth is one of the fundamental conditions for reaching economic equality.

Entrepreneurship · 7

MOST SUBORDINATE racial or ethnic groups are deficient in entrepreneurship, as, for example, the Afro-Americans and many Third World peoples. Entrepreneurship is difficult to measure; note instead that 8 percent of white Americans are self-employed, compared with 4 percent of black Americans. Programs for the development of entrepreneurship were created all over the world in the 1960s and 1970s, with the United States taking the lead. Yet controversy abounds both as to the objectives and as to the achievement of such programs.

A deficiency of entrepreneurship is bad for the image of a subordinate group. Entrepreneurs are one of the power units in the establishment, along with bishops, generals, landowners, and secretaries of state. A group without its share in each of these lacks prestige. Its image is deficient, and image matters, since there is much more image than substance in racial behavior. Image apart, the group is also low in power, because entrepreneurs wield substantial power, not only over those they employ but in society at large. Entrepreneurs also tend to hire disproportionately members of their own racial or ethnic group, so a deficit works against the group's getting its fair share of the better jobs. Presumably a deficit in entrepreneurship could be partially offset by extra dominance in something else, like the army or advanced science, but some sense of deficiency would remain.

The paucity of black entrepreneurship is not much more than a talking point in American politics, but in a number of other countries the extent to which business enterprise is concentrated in particular groups is a major source of racial conflict, even in some cases to the point of genocide. Such concentration existed in the Middle East, where Greeks, Armenians, and Jews predominated in trade, rather than Turks or Egyptians; in Southeast Asia, where Chinese were prominent in trade; in East Africa, where it was the Indians; in Nigeria, the Lebanese and the Ibos—to name the best-known cases. How to diminish the intensity of these conflicts is one of the world's most acute problems, and it has given rise to many programs for entrepreneurial development.

Interest in entrepreneurial programs is not confined to racial or ethnic situations. The topic concerns governments that would like to extend the public sector, for whatever reason. A major obstacle in many developing countries is the shortage of competent public managers, in consequence of which public-sector enterprises are poorly managed, in the sense that plants are operating far below capacity, materials are wasted, labor complements are excessive, and so on. Some governments find themselves encouraging foreign entrepreneurs to supply goods and services that they would prefer to supply for themselves, were it not for the inefficiency of government enterprise. Programs for the formation of a business cadre are therefore as important to socialist countries as to countries developing through private enterprise.

Some critics claim that business programs are unnecessary, for various reasons. One proposition, particularly relevant to the United States, argues that economic development will be sponsored mainly by large corporations, so if blacks want to play a leading role in the economy, it will be by becoming officers in large corporations rather than by setting up small businesses on their own. For this set of critics the slogan for encouraging blacks in business would be not "black capitalism" but "blacks in capitalism." The appropriate aid would be not low-interest loans, but scholarships to attend business schools. And the appropriate target, given that blacks constitute 10 percent of the labor force, would be that in Detroit blacks would not just be at the bottom of General Motors, but would find themselves filling 10 percent of the vice-presidential jobs, 10 percent of middle-management jobs, and so on all the way along the line.

I shall not pursue this line of argument for it asks us to choose between "either" and "or" when "both" would be appropriate. If blacks are to have 10 percent of everything, then they should have 10 percent of the jobs of vice-presidents and 10 percent of small and medium businesses. Some blacks want to be businessmen, and so long as this option exists for whites, it should also exist for blacks. One could not defend spending hundreds of millions of dollars just to create a handful of black millionaires, but a modest program targeted at small businessmen is no more unusual than any other educational program.

The second charge is that programs are unnecessary because, given market opportunities, the economic system will produce for itself as many entrepreneurs as it needs. Entrepreneurship, according to this thesis, is not exogenous but endogenous. If there seems to be a shortage of entrepreneurs, it is because the economic system is unprofitable, and does not indicate any deficiency of number or quality of entrepreneurs.

I wish that I could present a brief and clear statement of what economics has to say about the development of entrepreneurship, but unfortunately this is impossible. Entrepreneurship is one of the weakest and most confused parts of economic analysis. The reason is partly that entrepreneurship emerged in Europe before the spate of economic writing began to flow in the second half of the eighteenth century. Economists took entrepreneurship for granted—as something that is always there when it is needed. They did not begin to study the subject seriously until Max Weber asked: Where did all those entrepreneurs come from, and why are so many here and so few there, finding his famous answer in the emergence of the Protestant ethic. In placing his answer in this context Weber opened up the subject to sociologists, psychologists, geographers, and historians, no less than to economists, and thus launched a voluminous literature which flows unabated to this day. Entrepreneurship is therefore what we call a multidisciplinary subject. Sadly enough for those of us who are emotionally inclined to welcome multidisciplinary subjects, this one offers no evidence that the level of confusion and the level of multidisciplinariness are negatively correlated.

Economists fell behind not only because they took entrepreneurship for granted but also because they were slow to recognize how its character was changing over two centuries. Let us distinguish four groups of entrepreneurial functions: to supply capital; to organize production and marketing; to bear uninsurable risks; to conduct the firm's external relations.

The relative importance of these functions has changed over time. Early economists dwelled mainly on the first of these functions, the supply of capital, and always referred to the entrepreneur as "the capitalist." Distinguished names such as those of Adam Smith, David Ricardo, and Karl Marx are in this group. This made sense, because finding the necessary capital was a big headache for the small family business of early capitalism, just as it is now for new business in developing countries or in Afro-American circles. But today's entrepreneur in the large modern corporation (if one can find him) is not primarily a source of capital; he may own only a tiny fraction of the capital used in the business, and may leave it to his financial vice-president to worry about where money is coming from.

Size of enterprise is one of the major factors deciding the entrepreneur's role. In the small firm the second function of entrepreneurship—to organize production and marketing—is the top man's biggest task. But the large entrepreneur has specialists in accounting, in marketing, in personnel management, in industrial engineering, and so on to handle most managerial problems. The top man's task is to choose and manage his team of specialists, which calls for qualities of leadership rather than for specialized knowledge.

The upgrading of management to be a separate factor of production we owe to Alfred Marshall, writing at the end of the nineteenth century, with some slight debt to Richard Cantillon, J. B. Say, and J. S. Mill. But Schumpeter, who was an extremist, would not even admit that management was an entrepreneurial function, since he expected it to be done by hired hands. He concentrated on the third function, which he called innovation, but which I have included under the heading of uninsurable risk. I suppose that he would also now recognize the fourth function-the maintenance of external relations. This is a major new function in countries where businesses can take no step without a license to build, to import raw materials, to manufacture a product—and where good relations with ministers, civil servants, the press, and other molders of public opinion is essential to success.

Schumpeter's concentration on innovation brought useful insights into the way pioneers established themselves, especially at the end of the nineteenth century in Western Europe and the United States, but the device is not useful in the contexts that we are investigating. Outside the leading industrial countries entrepreneneurs do not pioneer in Schumpeter's sense. The most innovative of them import ways of doing things that have already proven their worth in leading countries and adapt them to suit local resources and domestic or export markets. The rest imitate their fellows, hoping to win a share of the rising demand. These tasks are arduous and challenging, and they are not lightened by the fact that people with managerial experience and know-how are in scarce supply for hiring. Schumpeter believed innovation to be the most important contribution of entrepreneurship in leading industrial countries. In the same spirit we might pick the managerial function as the most important in developing countries—or in the Afro-American community—since this is their most striking deficiency.

One conclusion gained from this analysis is that small-scale entrepreneurship is probably more difficult than large-scale entrepreneurship. Access to the necessary finance is more restricted; the entrepreneur's personal fortune is more at risk; and there is less help with managerial problems, since the firm is too small to hire a complement of skilled managers. If I may exaggerate a little, almost anybody can run General Motors, but it takes very special qualities to run a successful corner store. What is the nature of these qualities?

Max Weber launched the idea that the entrepreneur is a special kind of person, different from the rest of us, but elaboration of this theme had to await the intervention of the psychologists. The leading contribution is that of David McClelland. McClelland really starts from Schumpeter's grand innovators, so his listing of the characteristics of entrepreneurs makes them seem somewhat larger than life. But the approach is not irrelevant even to the small Marshallian businessmen on whom we have to focus, especially if the suggestion that their path is peculiarly difficult has merit.

McClelland's entrepreneurs are driven by the desire to excel; as he puts it, they need achievement. This distinguishes them from some other great men who are driven by a need for power. Achievers are few, but power-seekers are innumerable, and their ubiquity is the main reason that the world is such a violent place. People who need achievement have no marked love of power. They can also be distinguished from those who are motivated by a need for affection or recognition by the tribal group. These aim to please rather than to excel. Indeed American cynics say that the United States began to falter when American mothers switched from urging their children to get ahead to urging them to get along.

McClelland identifies several characteristics of achievers of which I shall emphasize only three. First, the achiever has a craving for excellence; he demands zero defect in his own performance and in that of others around him. Second, he listens carefully to criticism of his work, seeking ways to improve it. Most of us are like this in childhood, but the taste for criticism fades rapidly as we become adults—except in achievers. Third, achievers are highly self-disciplined; they practice incessantly, doing the same thing over and over again until they get it right.

We should note, however, that to be an achiever may be a necessary but is not a sufficient condition for success in business. Achievers are to be found in every walk of life, and most of them would fail in business. To succeed in business requires certain additional qualities.

First, one must desire to serve the public and be attentive to the customer's attitudes. This is not needed in a fly-by-night business, or for selling to passersby; but it is needed in setting up a manufacturing business which is to serve a regular clientele over the next fifty years. This need to respect one's public sets the businessman apart from many other achievers; you can be a great poet or surgeon or pianist and care nothing for public opinion.

Second, the good businessman must acquire a reputation for fulfilling all his contracts: paying his creditors on time; meeting delivery dates for his customers; honoring promises to his staff; and so on. A reputation for reliability is the competitive business' most valuable asset. As a background to this quality the businessman must have decisiveness; for if decisions are postponed, you cannot meet your contracts on time. "Mañana" is an excellent way of life for those who live off rental incomes, but it will not work in business.

The third quality is leadership. As the business grows in size, responsibility is delegated to sub-managers, and the entrepreneur becomes the leader of a team. The ability to choose good men and earn their affection and respect is a rare quality, especially in less-developed countries, where those in charge more often rely for obedience on fear and cruel punishment.

So far my characteristics have had a highly moral flavor; not so the fourth characteristic, which is a streak of ruthlessness. It does not pay in the long run to be ruthless with one's customers, suppliers, or staff, but it pays to be ruthless with competitors—to attract away their customers, undercut their prices, preempt their sources of raw materials, or buy them out. This ruthlessness is what the public dislikes, but in the emergence of great industries and great entrepreneurs, it is almost always central at critical moments in the story.

This list of characteristics of the business personality is not meant to be exhaustive. Neither is it implied that every successful businessman possesses all these qualities. I am painting an ideal type rather than a particular individual. I am merely establishing that it means something when one says that such and such a person is businesslike, and some other person is not. We thereby recognize that certain personality types are more likely to succeed in business than other types of personality. Experience also tells us that businesslike personalities are more common in some countries than in others, among some social or ethnic groups than in others, and at some historical times than at others. This is the core of the problem. Is the businesslike personality inherited or acquired? If acquired, in what environments does it flourish and multiply?

The role of inheritance need not detain us. No informed writer in this field has suggested that differences in entrepreneurship can be explained by genetic differences. Groups highly successful in business include Swedes, Ibos, Greeks, Parsees, and Cantonese—a wide selection of the human race; groups not remarkable in business include the Irish, French Canadians, Masai, Venezuelans, and Afghans—an equally wide selection.

Some genetic elements may be involved, but it is not unreasonable to assume that the number of people carrying these genes is much greater than the number of businessmen at any time, so that differences in business performance derive from differences in the proportions of the genetically qualified who enter business, rather than differences in the base. According to consensus, the quantitative differences in question have to do with culture, not with genes.

From this point on economists, psychologists, geographers, and sociologists diverge. Economists offer their traditional explanation—supply and demand. For most of them it is not possible for a society to be short of entrepreneurs in any basic sense. If opportunities for investment exist, entrepreneurs will emerge and seize them. If there are not many entrepreneurs, it is because there are not many opportunities. Even Schumpeter, whose entrepreneurs are giants, foresees no shortage of entrepreneurs if giant innovations are in the offing. To the economist the cause of an apparent shortage of entrepreneurs is usually to be found in governmental policies which make investment too risky or too unprofitable—in overvalued rates of exchange, in price control, threats of nationalization, high interest rates, excessive regulation, and so on.

Among the cases which have appealed to economic investigators have been the deceleration of the British economy in the last quarter of the nineteenth century and the rapid growth of factory industry in post-independence Pakistan. Social historians tend to explain the British case in terms of an ossifying third generation of industrial entrepreneurs, while economists have tried to prove with arithmetic that the entrepreneurs were wholly efficient, in the sense that they were maximizing profits, given the relative prices of labor and capital that they faced.

For a while the triumph of the economists was Pakistan. Here, before independence, the Muslims had shown no entrepreneurial tendencies, but with the disappearance of the Hindus and the establishment of a new structure that made investment profitable, a large number of Muslims emerged to create new industrial enterprises. Pakistan seemed to demonstrate that there could be a shortage of opportunities, but not of entrepreneurs. However, further examination showed that the new industrial entrepreneurs came from small and rather limited sects, raising once more the question why some groups produce relatively more people with businesslike personalities. The economists lost this round.

The psychologists are divided. The behavioral psychologists are close to the economists. Businesslike behavior is learned in response to systems of rewards and penalties; successful businessmen will be plentiful where it is rewarding to be a successful businessman. That is the behavioral school— essentially a variation of Pavlov's dogs. David McClelland led the child-rearing school. In this model one learns to be an achiever at one's mother's knee, in response to the kind of folktales she tells and the kind of heroes she favors. Achievers will be plentiful where the folktales idealize men who have faced difficulties that they have overcome by their own effort; whereas achievers will be scarce in societies where the folktales idealize brute force, or rank, or divine intervention. Fathers are important. A father who encourages his children to think for themselves and take initiatives stimulates creativity; whereas authoritarian fathers inhibit the development of entrepreneurship. Given that these personality traits are formed so young, and are in response to the stimuli of the older generation, it follows that to change the supply of entrepreneurs must take several generations. This is the original McClelland scheme, of which he now seems somewhat more doubtful.

This approach then raises the question, Why do some societies extol achievement more than others? What determines the orientation of the stories told at mother's knee? The economists' answer is again simple: the relationship between society and the achievement motivation is one of supply and demand. Societies that recognize and reward achievement get plenty of it, while those that distribute rewards on other bases tend to be low in personal achievement.

The upgrading of excellence in achievement as a basis for reward is relatively new in human history. It dates significantly only from the eighteenth-century Enlightenment, along with democracy, egalitarianism, the idea of progress, and other building blocks of modernization. Until that time the world accepted the premise that people should be rewarded on the basis of status. Good jobs went by family or class or religion. As exceptions one would reward a good singer or perhaps a good warrior, but mostly the plums were distributed by favor and not for performance. In such societies mothers do not hold up before their children the possibility of rising in life by excellence of achievement. Rising in life is not feasible. Instead one learns how to hold on to the little one has, how to acquire patrons, or even how to get by without being noticed by one's betters. After the Enlightenment we move into a different world, and the fact that some countries welcome achievement more than others is a natural consequence of the long time it takes for new ideas and ways of life to spread from pioneering countries to the rest.

A need for achievement is not enough to make a successful business personality. In my part of the world, the West Indies, there is high-achievement motivation for everything except business. We have produced the man the English say is the greatest cricketer in the world, and another man they say is the best novelist in the English language. We have great lawyers, surgeons, professors, calypso singers, and others, reared on self-discipline and the standard of zero defect. But our achievement in business is poor. This is because the business personality needs also the second set of characteristics I have outlined, especially the desire to serve and the reputation for reliability. Here also we find cultural lag. Top people in pre-Enlightenment societies do not think of themselves as servants. They expect to be able to break their contracts with impunity, and they rely on punishment rather than leadership to have things done their way. Most of the Third World needs the ideological transformation toward the ideal of service, which is associated with producing large numbers of persons with businesslike personalities.

This is the answer to those who, under the leadership of Ellsworth Huntington, have explained national differences in entrepreneurship not in terms of genes but in term of climate, arguing that temperate climates are more conducive to human endeavor than tropical climates, whether because of direct effects on human energy or because of the easygoing cultures which hot climates promote and demand. The proposition is indisputable for extreme ranges of climates; men do not function well in temperatures of 105° any more than in temperatures of 32°F; and in general the human race has avoided peopling such places in any considerable numbers. When we talk about tropical areas with large numbers of people, we are talking about India, Southeast Asia, West Africa, Brazil, and the northern parts of Latin America. This is a very large area about which to generalize. It includes many groups of people distinguished by high levels of performance and many others with lower performance. What they all share, apart from hot climates, are cultures that have not yet been fully permeated by the ideals of the Enlightenment. Until we can separate out the cultural elements, which the passage of time will do, we cannot say how much, if anything, is the result of climate.

The economists, the geographers, and the psychologists were comparing whole societies. So was Max Weber. But later sociologists have asked why within the same country different groups yield different proportions of entrepreneurship. The economist's answer does not suffice, because we get this differential performance even where government policy is the same toward all groups, as in West Pakistan. And even if one accepts the child-rearing hypothesis, the question remains of why the mothers of one group deliver a different message from the mothers of other groups in the same country.

Weber thought he had found the answer in religion, in the Protestant ethic as it shaped itself among the followers of Calvin. The tie to the Calvinists could not hold, partly because its logical foundations were insecure and partly because this so-called Protestant ethic is shared by some other kinds of Christians, including Quakers and Mormons, as well as by others who are not even Christian, such as the followers of Confucius and the Shintoists. However, this does not mean that there is no connection between religion and entrepreneurial performance, for groups which take pride in their entrepreneurial performance may well absorb into their religion the appropriate ethical foundations. The religious connection is then the result and not the cause of their success.

The trend of sociological writing since Weber focuses on the alien characteristic of those who are disproportionately successful in business. Entrepreneurs are seen to be "marginal" men, not fitting into established hierarchies. They may be former serfs, seeking refuge in the towns, as Pirenne saw them. Or younger sons in a society which practices primogeniture. They may belong to ethnic or religious minorities. Immigrant minorities are a common source of disproportionate entrepreneurship. This approach is very much in tune with what we see in developing countries, such as the entrepreneurial eminence of Germans and Japanese in Brazil, of Lebanese in West Africa, or Indians in East Africa, and of Chinese in Southeast Asia. But we also have notable nonimmigrant groups, like Ibos in Nigeria, Antioqueños in Colombia, Parsees in India, or the entrepreneurial sects in Pakistan.

It is easy to understand why minorities may thrive in business. The standard theory is that they move in this direction because, for reasons of race, religion, tribe, or what you will, they are excluded from other seats of power and influence. They cannot be bishops in the established church, or hold high rank in the army, or buy large landed estates and become aristocrats. Here and there an individual is adopted by the establishment, but his position remains ambivalent, and token. So the drive for achievement in such minorities pushes the young to compete in those sectors where performance is what counts and where social status is of little help. Notable sectors are athletics, the entertainment business, the world of scholarship, and the world of commerce. No sector is completely free from favoritism, but in these four the public will recognize superior merit, and will support it. Normally minorities begin with small businesses and move on from there, serving first their own communities, then moving out into the world beyond. Afro-Americans have taken over athletics, are laying siege to television, and are just now bursting into academic scholarship. Whether they will come to show equal vigor in business is the question. This group displays no lack of achievement motivation; the question is only along what channels it will be allowed to flow. The usual comparison with Indian, Chinese, and Japanese business success is not appropriate, since from 1650 until after the Second World War Afro-Americans were compelled to live and work with very restricted opportunities, whereas these Asian groups have had centuries of trading institutions and traditions behind them.

Immigrant groups do not achieve equal success everywhere. For one thing, the opportunities are not equal everywhere, and immigrants succeed better where the opportunities are greater. For example, the Italians took much longer to achieve economic equality in the United States than in Argentina, and West Indians seem to be more successful in New York than in London. The rapid economic growth of Argentina up to 1929 and the relative stagnation of Britain after 1960 are possible explanations.

Immigrants also differ in the extent of their own internal cohesion and self-support. In the most successful cases the extended family shares management and risk-bearing. This is particularly important in lines of business that require branches in different parts of the trading area (banking and wholesale distribution, for example). It also helps where a successful entrepreneur in one line decides to expand into other lines rather than to put more money into the existing enterprise. This is popular in the early stages of development, for it reduces risk and allows fuller utilization of experienced management. As he moves to develop new lines, he shifts the day-to-day control of the established businesses to relatives. In the absence of the extended family, other groupings can be used in the same way—for example, the village unit, formed as natives of the same village reconstitute their clan in the new world. Afro-Americans are not recent immigrants, but lack of cohesion is one of the more striking elements in their business performance; they might now be more successful if they had been allowed to retain their tribal affiliations. But one may also have excessive cohesion, where a rising businessman is required to provide scholarships, houses, cars, or businesses of their own, for his relatives, thereby depleting and stunting his own establishment. Immigrant groups also differ in their earlier level of economic achievement (the Cubans settling in Miami had more business experience before emigration than the Puerto Ricans settling in New York).

Success in business feeds upon itself and becomes a self-reinforcing process. Once this success begins to be noticed, in, say, an immigrant group, all the group's institutions adapt themselves in ways to serve the business personality. To be businesslike is absorbed into the religion, so religion reinforces such behavior. Mothers raise their children to be businesslike and start attributing the success of the group to the superiority of its religion, its customs, its history, or even its race. The group becomes clannish. Convinced that members of their group are more reliable than outsiders, they hire only their own people and prefer to give their business to their own people. Outsiders come to believe in the group's superiority. Bankers lend more readily to members of the group, and overseas suppliers prefer to use them rather than local businessmen as agents or as partners. The feedback process creates what is essentially a monopolistic situation, which makes it hard or even impossible for the native businessman to get a foothold.

The appropriate remedy for such a situation is some form of affirmative action. As long ago as 1484, Richard III, coping with an influx of religious refugees into, England decreed that a foreigner might take no other foreigner as apprentice, except his own son—thereby ensuring that the high industrial skills which these foreigners were bringing with them would be passed on to Englishmen. In 1523, Henry VIII amended this decree to prohibit foreigners from taking even their sons as apprentices. Modern counterparts of such legislation include limiting the number of foreigners to be employed in any particular business and decreasing this number at regular intervals, thus forcing the firm to hire and train nationals for positions at all levels.

Instead, many such situations have been allowed to come to boiling point. Armenians and Greeks have been driven out of Turkey, Indians out of Burma and East Africa, Nigerians out of Ghana and Zaire, and Ghanaians and Dahomeyans out of the Ivory Coast and Nigeria. Chinese have been murdered in Java, and Ibos murdered in Northern Nigeria. In less violent confrontations the foreigners have been allowed to remain but forced to sell their business to nationals. The case for affirmative action forcing the foreigners to hire nationals and impart their skills is beyond dispute; but the public loses when skilled foreigners are driven out before nationals have been trained to do the work. Affirmative action is better than mass murder.

The model in which minorities turn to commerce because, along with athletics, entertainment, and scholarship, it is a sector where competition ensures the triumph of merit, presupposes that the road is indeed open, and not blocked, whether by cumulative forces, such as I have just described, or by religious, racial, or other discrimination on the part of more powerful groups in the society. Such blockage is by no means uncommon. Presumably it, too, has cumulative effects. If people cannot borrow, or are not considered eligible for contracts or licenses, they perform badly. If they perform badly, they themselves, as well as others, will come to believe that they lack the qualities required for business, or the right culture, or the right religion. Their children will look in other directions, rather than to business. Thus, French Canadians pride themselves on their superior performance in the creative arts—literature, painting—and at the law, but have hitherto taken it for granted that success in business was not for them.

What subordinate groups need for successful entrepreneurship are opportunity, the business ethic, and time. Opportunity includes group cohesion and self-support, easy access to capital and to management advice, and affirmative action against exclusionary practices. The developing countries have business promotion packages of this kind. The business ethic includes meeting commitments on schedule and maintaining good relations with contacts. Time, because such behavior has to be learned. The economists are probably right that in the long run the economic system will produce all the entrepreneurs it needs, but this does not hold in the short run. In the less-developed countries the most successful trading groups are those in which son follows father (or other close relative) into the business, and is brought up to do so almost from birth. Such a son learns a tremendous amount about how to be successful in business which, while not impossible, is difficult to absorb in other ways. It is difficult but not impossible. It just takes longer.

Colonial Relations · 8

FROM THE ECONOMIC STANDPOINT, colonialism is a system for improving the terms of trade in favor of the metropolis. There have been other purposes. The word comes to us from the Greeks, who planted colonies of their own race, not for trade but to dispose of surplus population. Other metropoles have demanded annual tribute. The Spaniards went in search of precious metals. Colonies have been held for military purposes, as military bases. But by the end of the nineteenth century, trade was the central purpose of holding colonies, and more favorable terms of trade were the central expectation. Race is not a necessary element in colonialism, nor is forced labor.

Force becomes a necessary element if there is a shortage of labor to work with the colonial settlers, especially if the aboriginal inhabitants are wiped out, as in the Americas, Australasia, and parts of Africa. Then slavery is introduced, in its stronger or weaker versions, including indentured labor from India or China. If the colony is already well populated, it is not necessary to import labor. The government may force the farmers to deliver specified amounts of produce, as the Dutch did in Java; or trade with the natives may be relied on, if a regular flow of trade at favorable prices seems assured, as in West Africa at the turn of this century. Some investment in transport facilities may be required to open up the colony for easy movement of produce in and out. Prices may be manipulated, with ceilings placed on the prices of exports. Imports can be stimulated by keeping import tariffs low and discouraging local production of manufactures; down to the First World War the government of India bought supplies only in England and not from competing sources in India. Some colonial powers, notably France, made preferential arrangements, giving themselves special terms for imports or exports in preference to other trading nations. Some writers see India's market as a source of foreign exchange used by the British to balance their own triangular payments, but without India, Britain would have had to find other markets, so this is another aspect of the terms of trade.

Much is made of the colony's role as a source of strategic materials, and we would expect to find the search for raw materials playing a major role in the search for colonies. But this was not so in the heyday of colonialism, before 1914. Until then the only raw material the British were concerned about was cotton. In this century oil has played a significant role in Middle East politics; and chrome, we are told, is the principal tie binding the United States to the white side in the Union of South Africa. Control over raw materials is important in wartime; in peacetime it makes little difference if the international commodity markets are working normally.

An alternative explanation associates colonialism with a drive to invest on the part of imperial powers. Two different versions are given. In one, a deficiency of purchasing power leads to a surplus of goods in the imperial economy's market, with equilibrium restored only by overseas investment. It cannot be restored simply through more trade, because the surplus of goods is not reduced if extra exports are matched by extra imports. In the other version, profits fall as the economy matures, and saving is deflected to foreign investment in order to keep up the profits ratio. This will not occur if a steady flow of innovation produces a flow of profitable investment opportunities; it is therefore feasible for an economy in the lead, but not for a follower. Neither of the two leaders in foreign investment at the end of the nineteenth century, Britain and France, was technologically in the lead at that time, so their overseas investment levels could not have been forced on them by domestic maturity.

In any case, even if there were domestic forces driving these countries to invest overseas, it is not clear why they would decide to invest in underdeveloped areas. Some capital would be spent on opening up colonies with transportation facilities and other forms of investment that would bolster colonial exports of primary products and colonial imports of manufactures. Beyond this, there was little interest in investing in colonies, even if this yielded one percentage point more in interest, and indeed the bulk of foreign investment by metropolitan countries did not go to their colonies. We face the same situation today. A great deal of attention is paid to multinational corporations in the Third World. But in fact, apart from oil, most of the investment of such corporations is not in the Third World; it is in Europe and North America. Investment flows more naturally toward developed areas than to the less developed.

Race is not a necessary element in colonialism. Colonialism acquired a racial element when the Spaniards imposed themselves on the South American Indians in the sixteenth century, but most colonials were white in 1750, and white colonialism did not end until successive tides were turned by North American independence, by Latin American independence, the Monroe Doctrine, and the spread of nationalism in Central and Eastern Europe. By 1920 practically all European peoples had become independent, while practically all non-Europeans, with the exception of the Chinese and Japanese, were colonials. Colonialism, although not so originally, had become a racial system.

As the colonial system became more racial, it also became more racist. Small European military and administrative forces were required to govern vast territories, including hundreds of millions of people of different languages, religions, and customs. Thus, India was governed by an army that had only one soldier per thousand of population. This task was accomplished by means of a twofold strategy. First, the imperial powers attracted, allied themselves with, and supported local power centers that would work with them. Chiefs, kings, rich merchants, and mining companies were supported by the government and in turn supported it. Secondly, the doctrine of racial superiority was promulgated. There was to be no socializing between black and white, and the blacks were to be persuaded of the innate superiority of the whites. Thus, through fear, superstition, and ignorance, it became possible for handfuls of military and administrative white men to keep large numbers of indigenous peoples in subjection.

Such a system could be stable only if the natives could be kept out of secondary schools and universities. Where young people were receiving the same education as that of the rulers, while being denied employment in government jobs or big business corporations on grounds of color, resentment and frustration built up to levels where it could no longer be constrained. Whatever may have been the economic reasons for abandoning the colonies, the revolt of the young educated natives was an independent factor making its own explosion. This revolt had reached an advanced state in India; other colonies were at varying distances behind.

Metropolitan powers varied in their application of the color bar to native intellectuals and professionals. In West Africa the British disliked educated natives and refused to socialize with or hire them. Africans were not eligible for college-level positions in the British Territories, thus giving semblance to Bernard Shaw's gibe that the British Empire was a system of outdoor relief for the British middle classes. By contrast, in the colonies or at home the French treated educated Africans as fully French, gave them jobs, and married them to their sisters. Yet each policy was inconsistent. The French seemed to act without prejudice, but so little provision for native education at any level was made that it was easy to assimilate the few educated Africans. The British, on the other hand, encouraged the missionaries to provide education up to the secondary level and further encouraged Africans to train for professions—even while making it clear that on completion, they would not be employed in the government service. This caused frustration and anger. At independence, power passed to these educated people, with their affection for the French and their dislike of the English. This is one reason why France and her ex-colonies have collaborated closely over the past twenty years, whereas Britain and her African ex-colonies as well as India have drifted apart.

Another important difference is that the British kept working- or lower-middle-class persons out of their colonies, while the French flooded theirs with *petits blancs*. This was how the education system worked. The British missionaries provided enough education for Africans to fill most jobs at the secondary level, apart from skilled craftsmen. The French did not and imported French men and women for such low-level jobs as domestics, waitresses, shop assistants, and semi-skilled workers. Why this difference existed is not clear. Since France was short of labor, and importing labor from around 1890 onward, and since she trumpeted *la mission civilisatrice*, it is odd that she was so stingy with elementary and secondary education for her native subjects.

Did the colonial system pay the metropolitan powers? This is a hard question to answer. Of course it paid some individuals,

while others lost; and presumably those who won had disproportionate influence on the making of metropolitan policy.
The difficulty arises when one tries to assess profit and loss for
the country as a whole. Adding private and public returns,
did it make a profit or a loss on its colonies?

On the surface, each metropolis acquired millions of acres
of land, much of it desert, but some of it rich in gold or silver
or copper, and some to be bitterly disputed between incoming
white settlers and native occupants. Most of the acquisition
could not be developed without major infusions of capital.
These were for the most part not forthcoming. Depending on
the effort made, colonialism paid in some places but not in
others. It clearly paid the Dutch in Java during the period of
the Culture System, when produce requisitioned from farmers was sold at a net profit of $330 million (U.S.) over this per-
iod (1830–1870). It probably paid the British in India during
the second half of the nineteenth century, when the Indians
paid the entire cost of the Indian government as well as of
wars outside India fought by the Indian army. On the other
hand, it seems highly improbable that Spain made much profit
in the Philippines, or that Indochina yielded France any profit
comparable with the cost of the war of conquest. Who bene-
fited from settling Frenchmen as farmers in Algeria, or Englishmen in Kenya, would be hard to assess.

Earlier in this book I asked the question, Why does the
landowner exploit the tenant when it may be more profitable
to invest in developing his productive capacity? Part of the
answer is that many policies that would enrich the colony will
not benefit and may even harm the metropolitan power. The
latter is interested only in policies that improve his trade. Still,
this means that he is interested in agricultural and mineral development, and we would expect to find colonial governments active in this field. But this was not so. The Dutch were
very active in developing their colonies throughout the nineteenth century. The British were uneven, except in promoting
cotton cultivation and the plantation enterprises of Southeast
Asia (tea, coffee, rubber, sisal, and so on). France, active in

planting settlers in Algeria, was dormant elsewhere. The other metropolitan powers (Portugal, Spain, Turkey) were not interested in development at home, and reflected the same lethargy abroad. Colonialism is identifiable with neglect to an even greater extent than with exploitation.

But how about the terms of trade? Actually colonialism made little difference to the terms of trade, except insofar as it helped to keep supplies of colonial produce growing about as fast as demand; and the terms of trade made little difference to colonial income per capita, within the narrow range in which they moved. On top of all this the imperial governments held no unique opinion about terms of trade. The British wanted higher prices for coffee and rubber, which their colonies sold to the United States, and lower prices for tea and cotton, which their colonies sold to Britain. Strict identification of the terms-of-trade issue as a colonial versus metropolitan issue would therefore be misleading. Nevertheless, the topic lies at the heart of today's tensions between white and non-white nations.

The factors that determined the terms of trade for tropical produce had little to do with government manipulation in the form of tariffs, preferences, or other discrimination. The dominant element was the supply price of tropical labor in comparison with the supply price of labor in Britain and other industrial countries. Throughout the nineteenth century the supply price of tropical labor was less than a shilling a day for migrant labor, and as little as sixpence a day for labor in India. The price was determined presumably by the low marginal productivity of Indian farmers in growing food. Their annual output of food per farm person was about one-fifth that of a British farm worker. The factoral terms of trade, which is to say the ratio of British to Indian earnings, had to be no less than five to one.

About 30 million Indians emigrated between 1850 and 1930 to work in other tropical countries. Many millions of Chinese did the same. Employers in tropical countries could get all the cheap labor they needed, while employers in the temperate countries had to pay a multiple of these wages. These factoral terms of trade, then, set the relative prices of commodities, known as the commodity terms of trade.

This outcome did not depend entirely on Indian and Chinese migration. In any tropical country the farmer could choose between growing food and growing a commercial crop for export. If he produced for export he would expect to earn at least twice as much as if he grew food. (I assume twice as much to allow for extra risks or unfamiliarity with the export crop.) So one way or the other the basic determinant of the supply price for tropical labor or tropical produce would be the marginal productivity of the tropical food farmer. This continues today. The migration of Chinese and Indian labor on indentures has ended, but the low marginal productivity of food producers in the tropics still yields a low supply price for tropical labor.

Now suppose that the export crop is tea, and that productivity in tea doubles. Then its price will halve: twice as much tea will be needed for a fixed quantity of food. If the price does not fall by as much as half, more tea will be offered; if it falls by more than half, less tea will be offered. It follows that research designed to increase productivity in tea does not benefit tea producers. If successful, it merely reduces the price they get for tea. The terms of trade are fixed by the amount of food that the farmer could otherwise produce. In this model the farmers benefit if their own productivity rises in food, or if the productivity of the industrial countries rises in the goods that the farmers import, but the farmers gain nothing from greater productivity in their own exports.

This the colonial powers recognized. They spent a great deal of money on research into the commercial export crops— especially tea, cocoa, rubber, sugar, and oil palm—which yielded dividends in lower export prices, but they spent next to nothing on research in tropical foodstuffs. The large international research stations devoted to tropical foodstuffs were all created after 1950.

Third World leaders have attacked commodity prices as being immorally low; defenders of the status quo have responded that the prices are determined by demand and supply in open competitive markets and must therefore be correct. Essentially the sugarcane laborer says: "the sugar production in which I am engaged is one of the finest arts, embodying the latest in chemistry, biology, and engineering; no other industry is more advanced technologically. Therefore, I should earn at least as much as a steelworker. Instead, you tie my wage to that of the least advanced small farmer, offering me 700 pounds of grain, on the ground that this is what I would be growing if I were not producing sugar." The same argument is used by the women's movement. A woman's job, they say, should be rated according to the demands it makes on skills, strengths, and other qualities, when compared with the median man's job. Women should be paid according to the comparable worth of jobs measured by what is required of the performer, rather than by the supply price of an overcrowded market for female labor. "Not so," replies the market economist. "People are paid, and should be paid, according to their supply price and not according to the use that will be made of their labor." Actually the policy rule for internal trade is equal pay for equal work, it being assumed that departures from this would be eliminated by competition. But tropical producers receive instead pay based on alternative cost. The two rules give the same result in internal trade (discrimination apart), but equal pay for equal work does not operate in external trade because immigration is controlled. Neither rule is more "moral" than the other, except that alternative cost is sustained only by keeping immigrants out.

The situation is not static. The fact that tropical labor has a low supply price in comparison with temperate labor enables tropical labor to compete with the temperate world in everything that both countries can do, as long as the difference in productivity does not exceed the difference in wages. Ultimately the big difference in wages will force temperate countries to surrender to the tropical countries all subtropical agricultural crops, all labor-intensive manufacturing, and all those minerals where tropical production can supply world demand.

Sugar and cotton are good examples. Beet sugar has always cost more to produce than cane sugar; it has survived, therefore, in the temperate countries only with the aid of subsidies or protection. The case of cotton is more complex. Cotton production should not have survived in the United States after 1870. It was being produced in India, Brazil, Mexico, Egypt, and many other places, and the expansion of cotton in these countries was held down by cotton production in the United States. At the same time these countries held down wages in the American cotton regions. Productivity was higher in the United States, but not high enough, when combined with low wages elsewhere, to leave room for a reasonable wage for southern cotton growers. Why did the industry continue? Because black labor remained in the South instead of migrating to other parts of the country, where wages were much higher. It is not absolutely clear why black labor remained in the South, not starting its northward trek in significant numbers until the First World War. It was not illegal to emigrate to another state, though one might be harassed by the police. A high level of indebtedness tied people to their localities, as did uncertainty about jobs and housing at the other end. Emigration takes a long time to gain momentum because it usually depends on pathfinders who go first and prepare the way for those who follow. It was the certainty of jobs during the First World War that really started the mass migration of blacks. Meanwhile their failure to migrate had created a circular situation. These southern blacks had to accept low wages to meet other tropical wages, and at these low wages other tropical countries could not compete with them in growing cotton.

It was not necessary to "own" colonies in order to share in the fruit of colonialism. For insofar as colonial powers refrained from giving themselves preferences in the commodity markets, the terms of trade were the same for all. Denmark could buy tea at the world price and not concern itself with how that price came to be the world price.

Instead of fighting to win colonies, a country could simply struggle for nondiscrimination, which was agreed to at Berlin in 1885, though not then fully honored. The British had the biggest colonial area, and though they succeeded in controlling most of the brokerage and shipping and insurance charges, they were reexporting colonial produce throughout Europe at free market prices. The best reason for owning colonies was fear that other colonial powers would discriminate. If colonial markets were open to all countries on equal terms, the principal spur to intercolonial rivalry would be removed. By the end of the Second World War this principle was fully understood by the leading powers.

By 1920 relations between the white and the colored peoples were conducted entirely within the framework of the colonial system. Not so today; within a short period after the Second World War one colony after another became politically independent. There were political and economic reasons for the drastic change. For the British the crucial colony was India; if it was not worthwhile holding India, no other colony was worth holding. Were there economic reasons in 1945 for holding India? The country had been declining since the First World War; national income per head was probably lower in 1947 than it had been in 1911. Throughout the nineteenth century the British had striven to hold down Indian manufacturing, especially of cotton textiles and of iron, but by 1913 even these constraints had been thrown off. It is doubtful that the ability to manipulate India's terms of trade had ever been worth much; the economic forces we have examined kept the terms of trade unfavorable to India anyway; the colonial system would make little difference to this. Perhaps it was possible to squeeze economic gains out of colonialism in 1900, but by 1945 the developed countries had decided against preferential manipulation of colonial prices. A few colonies were thought to have value as military bases, and interest in oil sources was growing, but in 1945 these were not yet the obsessions that they later became.

India's economic problems were more difficult than those of many other colonies, but India was relatively free from what would in practice be the most difficult problem in decolonization: what to do about the European settlers. This complication arose from the fact that the Europeans had acquired the best lands, in terms of rainfall and soil fertility, and had in force policies that stimulated an adequate flow of cheap native labor. In many cases the settlers had become the effective government of the colony, and they were especially prone (more so than the urban whites) to discrimination in social relations and in employment. The settlers were a major source of conflict. If not protected, they would probably be driven out and, not being able to take either the land or their houses with them, would have lost their principal capital.

What would the metropolitan governments do for the settlers? Would they just write them off? This was what Britain did in East and Central Africa, after testing the water in Kenya and learning that even small guerrilla groups could reduce government almost to a standstill. France took longer to learn, and bloodied herself in Algeria and Indochina; but she learned. Belgium and Portugal took longer still, and ultimately made the most destructive transfers to their successors. The Union of South Africa will be the last to learn, but its time has not yet come.

One major problem remained in 1945. I said that by the end of the Second World War the colonial system had lost its function as a protector of imperial powers against each other's policies. However, its function as a protector of the property of investors against predatory acts, public or private, remained, and the abandonment of the system, in the years immediately following the Second World War, implied some degree of confidence that the successor states would assume these protective functions. This outcome could not be guaranteed. Leaders of the new governments came to power by denouncing colonialism in general and their former colonial power in particular. Investors were close to the old governments and had in many cases intervened against the politicians who were now in power; they were suspect and open to attack. In the new situation the corporations had money but little political power, and the ministry had power but little money. Ways of bringing money and power together were worked out, resulting in what is sometimes called neocolonialism, because some part of the role of the former governments has been inherited by the corporations instead of by the ministers.

The system has not worked smoothly, or all in one direction. There have been major battles some of which the corporations have lost—in Peru, Zambia, Guyana, and elsewhere. As a result of such battles the flow of foreign investment into Third World countries has declined, to the point where in the next decade a shortage of some minerals is possible. A United Nations committee has been designing a code of behavior for multinational corporations since 1977, but progresses slowly. Ultimately some modus vivendi will be reached because the two parties have the same interests: the corporations to dig more minerals and the governments to have the additions to national income generated thereby. Joint private and government explorations are the most likely step.

Aftermath of Independence · 9

MORE THAN one hundred countries have become independent and have joined the United Nations since the Second World War. This has changed significantly relations between white and non-white people, if only by sometimes giving the latter a power to be heard that did not exist before. Discussion of economic matters in international bodies seldom turns on racial differences, even where all the parties are aware of the racial implications; it is also true that many of the points in dispute would be disputed just as much even if all the parties were white. In addition to changes deriving from political status, changes in the marketplace have affected relations between rich and poor states; these did not necessarily derive from independence.

Seen from the viewpoint of potential change, the most important development in economic relations between rich and poor countries has been the working out of the consequences of different countries' having significantly different wage levels. This has operated at four points: mass migration to the industrial countries; the brain drain; the export of manufactures from less-developed countries to more-developed countries; and the export of primary products.

The mass migration of working-class people to the industrial countries resulted from a combination of population explosion in the developing countries and the exhaustion of the reservoirs of surplus labor in the developed. The population explosion led to an exodus from the countryside in search of work in the towns, since the towns were where job opportunities were expanding most. It has therefore put pressure on jobs in urban areas and stimulated willingness to migrate overseas—if further stimulus were needed.

The demand side resulted from the exceptionally fast pace of growth of Western European economies from 1950 onward. This led to a large transfer of workers from less-paid to better-paid jobs. The reservoirs of surplus labor were drawn down. Labor flowed out of agriculture, domestic service, retailing, small-scale trucking, and small-scale manufacture. Service jobs gave way to self-service in shops, hotels, restaurants, and other labor-intensive industries. The household was mechanized, and women poured into the labor market. Despite all this, there was an acute shortage of labor, met by bringing in workers from the Mediterranean, the Caribbean, and Asia.

This immigration had significant effects. On the economic side, it helped keep down wages at the bottom of the wage hierarchy, and probably also at the top. Profits were larger and the system grew faster. The standard of living probably rose, for faster growth more than made up for a lower starting point. This cannot be established because we do not know what would have happened to wages and profits if the immigration had not occurred.

On the social side, the results were less happy. The new-comers were resented by the native labor force. Even where they were of the same race, like the Yugoslavs in Germany, ethnic differences brought conflict. Even the Finns were resented in Sweden. These resentments did not turn primarily on wages. They resulted from the need to share scarce physical resources—housing, hospital beds, school places—and differences in culture—noise levels, dating habits, clothes.

The British were the most perturbed by this migration and took the earliest steps to stop it, cutting down the rights of colonials and ex-colonials in a series of laws from 1961 onward. They abandoned the goal of a raceless society and adopted the homogeneous goal instead. They argued that their problem was more difficult than that of the Northwest Europeans, who were taking in Southern Europeans, while the British were taking in mostly Asians and West Indians, who were presumably more difficult to absorb culturally. Anyway, with the onset of recession in 1974 the continental immigration also ceased. And we cannot guess whether it will be resumed when prosperity returns.

In the United States supply has been more powerful than demand. In comparison with the European economy, the American economy has grown rather slowly since the mid-1950s. In fact, its reservoirs of cheap labor were filling up rather than emptying, because of the slow growth of the better-paid industries and occupations. The large influx of Hispanics, and especially of Mexicans, was caused not by a labor shortage in the United States but rather by population explosion in Latin America. This has resulted in the same antagonisms at the working-class level. But the employers back migration strongly, and it is likely to continue.

The 1970s brought another mass migration, to the Middle East from the Islamic world. Oil-exporting Middle East countries found themselves with a great deal of money after raising the price of oil in 1973. Accordingly, they launched large development programs and imported labor to implement them.

These movements of people were welcomed by the governments of the emigrants' countries, where remittances quickly became a major source of foreign exchange.

The second consequence of the gap between wages and salaries is the emergence of the brain drain. Until the end of the Second World War the graduates of higher education moved from developed to developing countries; now the movement is in the reverse direction. Apart from a few LDCs with large numbers of graduates who cannot find work, this migration is viewed with antagonism, whereas the working-class migration was seen as good fortune.

What has caused this brain drain? One reason is that race prejudice is much reduced nowadays in filling college-level jobs in the developed countries. A second reason is the establishment and multiplication of institutions in the developing countries, which are pouring out graduates. This has altered salary ratios. Under the colonial system professional salaries were higher in colonies than in Europe; now the gap has narrowed, or even in some places reversed itself. A third reason is that many of these graduates find conditions uncongenial in their own countries. The institutions in which they work there are not adequately equipped or, owing to nepotism or other patronage, are badly run. Others have become accustomed to the life style of the OECD countries, including escape from the demands of the extended family, and prefer the anonymity of life in Chicago or Milan.

There is talk of reducing the outflow, by denial of passports, and talk of taxing those who have left. The shortage of university graduates in LDCs is probably temporary, since all developing countries are building more post-secondary institutions than they need economically; soon they, like India, the Philippines, or Egypt, will regard the export of intellectuals as a valuable source of foreign exchange. Meanwhile the outflow performs an important function: it forces the authorities to try to understand the problems of this new class and to give some priority to solving these problems. Such a reaction does not come naturally, partly because politicians distrust intellectuals and partly because attacking intellectuals is considered a way to win mass votes.

The receiving countries, in turn, are becoming dependent on this flow. All over the world Indians, Filipinos, and Egyptians are the backbone of the hospitals' staff of residents, and science laboratories are on the same trend. This improves the image of Asians in the Western countries. Some of the disdain that white people have for the non-white peoples derived from the belief that only whites could achieve technological modernization. This belief is no longer tenable. Moreover, white and non-white scientists grow closer together all the time because they research the same problems, thereby bringing to race relations a perspective different from that of people concerned mainly with economic and political power.

As was noted in Chapter 8, the wage gap should allocate to LDCs all commodities where the gap in incomes exceeds the gap in productivity—whether we refer to primary goods or to manufactures. In primary products this was frustrated by restrictions imposed by MDCs to protect their farmers against exports from LDCs. These could be quotas on imports or tariffs. Or there might be subsidies. One may also include here tariff structures that tax raw produce lightly, while taxing heavily the same product after it has been refined. Such a tariff protects not the farmers but the refiners. LDCs have attempted to have these restrictions reduced or eliminated, but without success.

The fourth and most crucial change in LDC external economic relations since 1950 has been the export of manufactures from the developing countries to the industrial countries. The industrialization of the Third World progressed rather slowly from the last quarter of the nineteenth century, partly because colonial powers impeded it and partly because, as in Latin America, in those days decision makers tended to believe the propaganda that Europe and the United States had a comparative advantage in manufacturing. These ideas were finally rejected by 1950, and rapid industrialization began to substitute for imports.

It soon turned out, however, that even with import substitution a developing country's market for manufactures was too small to support much industrialization, so a few bolder spirits began to export to the world market—especially textiles and especially to Western Europe and the United States. This of course was an enormous market, permitting growth at previously unknown rates—10 percent per annum and more.

After a while the industrial countries began to feel the pinch. Taken as a fraction of total consumption of manufactures, imports from developing countries were negligible. Even now in the United States they account for only 2 percent of consumption of manufactures. But this 2 percent is concentrated in a small number of industries, where the effect cannot be ignored. People were becoming unemployed, and the protests reaching the legislatures were voluminous. Beginning in 1961, the developed countries began to impose quota restrictions on imports of textiles from LDCs. The restrictions were not very effective at first, but since 1974 the loopholes have all been stopped. The developing countries have steadily widened the range of their exports. Machinery now exceeds both textiles and clothing.

Exports of manufactures now are 35 percent of the exports of the oil importing LDCs. They will continue to grow rapidly, especially when the world economy as a whole resumes a fast pace. It is true that some industrialists in every developed country are opposed to letting in low-wage goods. On the other hand, to import cheap goods is a substitute for importing cheap labor. It frees wage labor from the low-wage occupations, permitting its transference to high-paying occupations, and thereby facilitating fast growth. The greater the resistance to immigration, the stronger should be the tolerance of cheap imports.

The future of LDC exports of manufactures will depend very much upon the state of trade. In part the demand will be greater when times are more prosperous; and in part the industrial countries will be more tolerant when it is easy to place displaced workers in expanding trades than when it is not.

The issues examined so far in this chapter resulted from the working of supply and demand in the market, given the wide gap between developed and developing country incomes per head. The LDC governments have raised many more. The most important is the terms of trade. We saw in the preceding chapter that these are determined by alternative costs to tropical farmers and that the prices farmers receive from export crops are low because their output of the domestic crops is low per head.

The remedy is inherent in the analysis. Raise the productivity of the farmers in foodstuffs and they will demand higher prices for their export crops. This assumes that the farmers will not simply be driven bankrupt by a glut of supplies, but the historical record shows that, as productivity rises, the number of farmers declines relatively and the urban population grows. Demand thus grows with supply. Raising productivity, however, takes time.

Currently LDCs are proposing an international agreement for each major agricultural product or mineral, with each agreement providing inter alia for a buffer stock of the commodity. These stocks would stabilize prices, reduce inflation, and circulate purchasing power in an anti-cyclical rythmn. The buffer would thus benefit both buyers and sellers, if its administrative problems could be overcome.

Officially the buffer stocks are always proposed as stabilizers, but in practice the suspicion persists that they may be used to raise the average level of prices. Because in the past schemes that raised prices increased supply and cut demand, it is feared that these agencies would collapse under a burden of rising stocks and diminishing cash.

The simplest way to raise the price of a commodity would be for all producing countries to impose an export tax on it. Farmers would automatically find it more profitable to cultivate alternatives, so its price would rise by almost the full amount of the tax (subject to the elasticity of supply). This solution is the easiest to administer because it eliminates both country and producer quotas and does not require buffer stocks or annual decisionmaking. But it requires the participation of producer countries; otherwise those who abstained would attract larger shares of the trade.

Another important topic raised by LDC governments is the need for a code of behavior for multinational corporations. Again this is not a racial topic, since the countries receiving private foreign investment include Canada, Australia, and the Netherlands, whose approach to the question parallels that of LDCs. It is of course the right of any country to pass laws governing the operations of foreign firms within its territory. But this is not enough, for the road is left open to play one country off against another. To avoid this all must take the same stand.

In practice the outcome of this argument has to be a compromise, especially for mining operations, because the governments of developing countries want the money just as badly as the corporations want the minerals. If no compromise is made, a wider issue must be faced. Who has the right to decide whether the earth's resources shall be used, and who may be denied access?

Are other nations entitled to buy the product, at a reasonable price? This was denied when in 1973 the United States government, facing a poor soybean harvest, restricted the export of soybeans, thus causing livestock in many countries to die prematurely for lack of feed. When the oil producers instituted their boycott later in the same year, they were claiming the same right to deny access. The liberal view is that all should have access at freely determined market prices. But not everyone accepts the morality of free market prices. Neither do those who say that "the earth is the Lord's," which could be interpreted as meaning that royalties for superior resources should go not into national pockets but into an international fund. Some such decision has already been made for the mining of the seabed. The questions of access may soon come to the fore, if the current dearth of investment in mining in the Third World produces a shortage of minerals and high prices; temperate countries may then demand the right to enter and mine, on payment of reasonable wages and royalties. The questions may also surface with regard to world food supplies. If the USSR, China, India, and Africa continue to be major importers, the right of American farmers to benefit from this in very high food prices would be questioned all around the world, even if market prices were seen to be completely free.

Finally there is the question of financial transfers from rich to poor countries. Concessionary finance rose swiftly in the 1950s, grew less rapidly in the later 1960s, and has rallied in real terms for the past decade or so. In the 1970s and 1980s the financial situation has been dominated by the eightfold increase in the price of oil. Huge short-term debts were built up by oil exporters as well as importers, and now several large debtors are unable to meet their commitments.

Action is needed at two levels. One is to reschedule debt and eliminate the prospect of widespread default. This will almost certainly be accomplished, for the governments of the lending countries do not want their banking systems compromised by the insolvency of their loans. At the second level financial institutions must be persuaded to continue lending to finance current transactions. The alternative would force LDCs to cut their investment programs and import less from the industrial countries. Because LDCs take about one-quarter of the exports of manufactures from industrial countries, any reduction in LDC imports would hurt business in the developed countries. But banks do not want to lend more money to debtors who are already overcommitted, so they will not easily be persuaded to comply with this part of the program.

The LDCs decided in the early 1970s that the best way to proceed was to demand a New International Economic Order and to have a grand confrontation with the industrial countries in the United Nations. A list was drawn up of all the matters to be considered, and a General Assembly resolution called for a set of special meetings to discuss and determine the new order. The General Assembly was chosen as the venue since in that body each country has only one vote, which is not the case in other international bodies.

The strategy did not succeed. The United States, Germany, and Britain denied the right of the General Assembly to decide issues that belong to other international organizations, such as The General Agreement on Trade and Tariffs (GATT), the International Monetary Fund (IMF), or the Food and Agricultural Organization (FAO), so the discussion broke down on procedure before it even got started. This disillusioning experience reopened thinking on strategy. LDC leaders are likely to conclude that they should pursue the suggestion of the industrial countries that the matters at issue be discussed and decided in the UN specilized agencies rather than in the General Assembly. The confrontation will then not be so spectacular, and the results will be some distance short of original hopes, but some progress may be made here and there.

The gap in income per head between LDCs and MDCs is so large that LDCs cannot plan their relationships with LDCs in terms of power; they must rely on influence rather than on power. Real per-capita income in Northwest Europe is about eight times as large as real per-capita income in, say, Sri Lanka, an island that has been within the modern world economy for a century and a half. The gap has widened all the time. A hundred years ago the difference would have been three to one, not eight to one. But whereas per-capita income grew at about 2 percent a year in Western Europe from, say, 1850, tropical incomes grew only at about 1 percent a year. After 1955 the growth rates were spectacular for a while, until the international recession that began in 1973. In the developing countries as a whole the growth rate of real per-capita income jumped to 2½, but the industrial countries also upped their rate to 3½ percent, so the 1 percent difference in growth rates remained, pushing up the incomes of industrial countries faster than the incomes of the poorer countries.

The principal culprit in this widening is not productivity but population growth. If we take growth rates of production in each sector separately (industry, agriculture, and services), the developing countries were growing faster than the industrial countries in industry and services, and only slightly slower in agriculture. Their overall growth rates were about the same: 5 to 5½ percent. The wide gap in income per head results from the much faster population growth in the developing countries, around 2½ percent a year, compared with 1½ percent in the industrial countries.

Fast population growth eats up resources. One builds schools, water supplies, hospitals, and factory space, only to find after twenty years of feverish activity that the number of persons lacking even elementary service is larger at the end than it was at the beginning. Population growth also puts pressure on food supplies, and if agricultural output fails to grow with demand, creates a growing shortage of foreign exchange. The gap between the rich and the poor countries will not start to narrow until the poor countries get their flood of population under control.

We must not think of developing countries as if they were all the same. Some of these countries live on the verge of famine, while others consume twice as many calories per day. Some have negative growth rates; others, like Thailand, Colombia, or Ivory Coast, are among the fastest growing countries in the world. Although the gap between the averages of developing and industrial countries will continue to widen for some time, some of the developing are catching up, just as Japan caught up over the last thirty years.

The majority of LDC governments now recognize that, however generous or mean the industrial countries may turn out to be, the major effort for development has to be made by the developing countries themselves, partly through better

use of their own resources and partly through more cooperation and trade with each other. The potential for fast growth
exists. The developing countries are capable of feeding themselves, given appropriate policies, have surpluses of basic raw
materials, and have begun to create their own heavy engineering industries. This is the basis of the strategy known as collective self-reliance, which was endorsed in the same General
Assembly resolution that called for a new economic order, but
which has not been pressed with comparable vigor. Recent re-
views of economic potential have strengthened the LDC leaders' sense of independence and self-confidence. They will not
give up the effort for a new international order, but they are
beginning to show that they know that with or without help,
the developing countries can succeed on their own.

Postscript

I CONCLUDE this small volume with a few reflections on the future of race relations that have emerged in the course of preparing it. They are not systematic. Some things that are obvious have been left out; others, of more interest than importance, are included. I shall begin with the more disheartening and move to the more encouraging phenomena.

First is the ubiquity of racial conflict on this planet. The racial situation is better in North and South America now than it was in, say, 1960; everywhere else in the world the reverse is true. Wherever it occurs, race conflict is bitter, ruthless, and murderous. In this respect it is not to be measured on the same scale with class conflict, which is much less widespread and not so violent.

Another disappointment is the bias of the free competitive market, which works against subordinate racial or ethnic groups in some situations—for example, where the task requires qualities that take two generations to learn, or where recruitment for the better jobs is by personal recommendation, or where trade is dominated by a single race. The need for affirmative action is not solely American; the same problems arise in Asia or Africa.

One of the more troubling aspects of the need for affirmative action derives from the imperfection of the labor market, so that recruitment into the better jobs, in-service training, and promotion depend at each stage on personal recommendation. Here the concept of the dual labor market has proved insightful. Where the recommenders all belong to the dominant group, members of the subordinate group are handicapped by lack of personal ties to those who control entry and, even if recruited, are not likely to receive equal treatment at all stages leading to further promotion. Market forces need institutional support.

In international relations the fear of the backlash stands out as an obstacle to the richer countries' helping the poorer countries: the fear is that the development of the poorer will result in a flood of cheap manufactures into the world market at the expense of one or more of the richer countries. The argument that for every extra dollar of manufactures that they sell, LDCs will also import an extra dollar of manufactures does not cope with the reallocation of jobs and infrastructure that such changes impose.

Now to more cheerful particulars. Racism is powerful, but market forces are powerful too; and, despite the reservations made, they work on the side of desegregation, when allowed full play. As we have seen in the United States, ever since 1950 the black labor force has been moving upward, toward parity with the white labor force. The immediate future cannot be predicted because great changes in supply and demand have been affecting the black labor force. On the demand side, the disappearance of one million black jobs in farm work; on the supply side, the boom in young persons entering the labor force, the great influx of women, and the flood of undocumented aliens. All of these had a negative effect on unskilled labor. Much of this will not be repeated, and a shortage of un-skilled labor could easily develop over the next decade, to the advantage of the black labor force. The outcome depends also on whether the American economy revives and maintains a fair speed over the next twenty years (say, 5 percent per annum). It depends also on immigration.

A theme that runs through this book is the dependence of desegregation on fast growth of the economy. This is the lubricant that makes it possible for the share of American blacks in above median jobs to increase without provoking impregnable resistance. This enables the industrial countries to buy more cheap manufactures from the LDCs in spite of the painful relocations that this may require. This is what maintains commodity prices that would collapse below their long-run trend if demand were not keeping pace with supply. The disadvantaged and the subordinate have a vested interest in fast economic growth. Every reduction in the target rate for economic growth is also a reduction in the strength of equalizing forces.

The prospect for economic growth is obscure. Growth is cyclical, so the poor performance of the last ten years may now be followed by some years of good performance. But longer-term trends—connected with changes in technology, or experiments in monetary policy, or new rules for fiscal policy—may even darken the short-term prospect, let alone longer outcomes.

In the end, economics is not enough. People of different races, religions, and cultures have to learn to live peacefully with each other, and to develop pluralistic and federal institutions where this is the only way. Economic progress will help decisively, but racism has its own deep psychological springs that must be drained directly. To learn to live peacefully with each other is going to take a long time.

Suggested Readings

Chapter 1. Economic Inequality

John Rex provides a short introduction to the study of race relations in *Race Relations in Sociological Theory* (London: Routledge and Kegan Paul, 1983). A more advanced guide is the set of essays sponsored by UNESCO under the title *Sociological Theories: Race and Colonialism* (Paris: UNESCO, 1980; New York: Unipub, 1981). Melvin Tumin makes a geographical tour of race relations throughout the world, in Melvin M. Tumin, ed., *Comparative Perspectives on Race Relations* (Boston: Little, Brown, 1969). See also Charles Issawi, *An Economic History of the Middle East and North Africa* (New York: Columbia University Press, 1982).

Chapter 2. Interracial Goals

The hard questions here are affirmative action and pluralism. The case for and against affirmative action is weighed by Alan H. Goldman, *Justice and Reverse Discrimination* (Princeton: Princeton University Press, 1979). Crawford Young offers a general survey of pluralism in *The Politics of Cultural Pluralism* (Madison: University of Wisconsin Press, 1976). Carl Friedrich makes a geographical tour in *Trends of Federalism in Theory and Practice* (New York: Basic Books, 1973). On education, see Brian M. Bullivant, *The Pluralist Dilemma in Education* (London: Allen and Unwin, 1981).

Chapter 3. Investment in Underdeveloped Groups

The Brandt Commission argues that it pays the rich countries to invest in the poor (dividends and interest apart). See Willy Brandt and Anthony Sampson, eds., *North-South: A Program for Survival. Report of the Independent Commission on International Development* (Cambridge, Mass.: MIT Press, 1980). The economics of education is scrutinized by various papers in J. E. Vaizey and E. A. G. Robinson, eds., *The Economics of Education* (London: Macmillan, 1966).

Chapter 4. Discrimination in Employment

Gary Becker, *The Economics of Discrimination* (Chicago: University of Chicago Press, 1957; rev. ed. 1971). Ray Marshall, "The Economics of Racial Discrimination: A Survey," *Journal of Economic Literature,* September 1974. Peter Doeringer and Michael J. Piore, *Internal Labor Markets and Manpower Analysis* (Lexington, Mass.: D. C. Heath, 1971). Orley Ashenfelter and Albert Rees, *Discrimination in Labor markets* (Princeton: Princeton University Press, 1974). Lester Thurow, *Generating Inequality* (New York: Basic Books, 1975. Raymond Loveridge and A. L. Mok, *Theories of Labour Market Segmentation* (The Hague: Martinus Nijhoff, 1979).

Chapter 5. Upward Mobility

Estimates of earnings by race and sex are published annually by the Bureau of the Census, Current Population Reports, Series P-60, *Money Income of Households, Families and Persons.* Figures for 1980 are given in No. 132. Occupational data by race, sex, and other characteristics are in United States Bureau of Labor Statistics, *Employment and Earnings,* monthly. The interpretation of some of the figures is disputed by those who wish to use them to establish how much or how little economic progress blacks have made over the past three decades. See Joseph R. Washington, Jr., ed., *The Declining Significance of Race?* (Philadelphia: University of Pennsylvania, 1979); Richard B. Freeman, *Black Elite* (New York: McGraw-Hill, 1977). Philip Blair, *Job Discrimination and Education* (New York: Praeger, 1972), is an excellent study of Hispanic Americans.

Chapter 6. Unemployment

Readings for this chapter are the same as those for Chapters 4 and 5.

Chapter 7. Entrepreneurship

Peter Kilby, *Entrepreneurship and Economic Development* (New York: Free Press, 1971). Albert O. Hirschman, *The Strategy of Economic Development* (New Haven: Yale University Press, 1958). Ivan Light, *Ethnic Enterprise in America* (Berkeley: University of California Press, 1972). J. S. Mangat, *Asians in East Africa* (Oxford: Oxford University Press, 1969).

Chapter 8. Colonial Relations

Both sides of the controversy initiated by Ronald Robinson and John Gallagher as to the motives of British imperialism at the end of the nineteenth century are well represented in W. Roger Louis, ed., *Imperialism* (New York: Franklin Watts, 1976). Benjamin Cohen, *The Question of Imperialism* (New York: Basic Books, 1973), ranges over the whole field. See also D. K. Fieldhouse, *Colonialism, 1870–1945* (New York: St. Martin's Press, 1981).

Chapter 9. Aftermath of Independence

W. R. Cline, *Policy Alternatives for a new International Economic Order* (New York: Prager, 1979). Donald Keesing and Martin Wolf, *Textile Quotas against Developing Countries* (London: 1980). Roger D. Hansen, *Beyond the North-South Stalemate*, (New York: McGraw-Hill, 1979).

Index